Sweet & Spicy

Arian Mabe

Copyright © 2023 Arian Mabe.

Some stories in this collection have been previously published as eBook singles and as part of a collection under the author's alternate pen name, Alis Mitsy.

All rights reserved. This book or any portion thereof may not be reproduced or used in any manner whatsoever without the express written permission of the publisher except for the use of brief quotations in a book review.

None of this book, in writing or editing, has been produced using generative AI. I do not give permission for this book to be used to train any AI models.

First printing, 2023.

https://arianmabe.wordpress.com/

This is a collection of short stories focusing on straight erotic encounters and romance. Pairings include anthros with anthros and also anthros with humans.

This collection of stories includes anal sex, first time play, BDSM, bondage, risky sex, impregnation and multiple partners.

Cover art illustrated by verysweetpotato; they are contactable via Twitter for work enquiries.

twitter.com/AlexandrCorvin

Table of Contents

Cherry Popping	5
Breaking Free	16
Finally	27
Purity Bound	35
Eaten Out on a Work Call	52
Aquatic Pleasure	63
The Werewolf's Lover	71
Cream-Pie Slut	79
Public Bondage	93
Storm Mating	101
Going for a Ride	123
Bondage & Impregnation	131
Dystopian Passion	140
Study Break	148
Breeding the Librarian	159
Breeding the Leopardess	170
Taking it Deeper	181
Lust in the Surf	193

Cherry Popping

The mare writhed on his bed, dark lips agape in a silent moan. After all, it was not as if Cherry had breath left in her lungs to moan aloud as her human lover's tongue and lips went to work between her thighs. His tongue lashed her pussy as she soundlessly gasped and arched her back, her strawberry roan coat struck through with red, brown and white hairs, creating an almost mottled, speckled effect. The sheets, twisted around Cherry's body, obscured her paler stomach, the white stretching up over her breasts, nipples pert and pink, standing up erect as her arousal grew.

Oh...and he was good at eating her out too. Cherry bit her lower lip, although there was nothing delicate about it as her marehood squeezed down on his thrusting fingers, her brown-haired lover intent on bringing her to an earth-shattering climax before he even thought about himself. He'd left his hair long enough for her to twist her fingers into it too and she hissed through clenched teeth, the rush of air escaping her in a burst of sound even as her nostrils flared, teetering on the breath-taking edge of a climax that she was so very sure would not be her last of the night.

But the mare knew one thing even as Isaac grunted into her sex, fingers digging deliciously into her soft, full thighs. She'd known it right when she'd trotted up to his dorm room, a bottle of liquor hidden in her handbag (well, the things were getting rather oversized these days) and a hopeful smile lighting up her muzzle. And she'd known it too when he'd taken her into his arms and kissed her with such a trembling passion that she could not help but melt into his embrace and know, in her heart of hearts, that he loved her truly above all else.

Cherry was ready.

Her cries most likely disturbed others in the dorm but neither of them had the strength of will to care in the heat of the moment, putting stock in the hope that most of them, at least, had returned home for the holidays, the light flurry of snow outside the window not enough to stick but enough to make everything feel just a little bit more Christmassy than the slouching tree in the courtyard belayed. It was okay that they were not home for Christmas, however – as long as they had one another to keep warm with.

Cherry panted heavily, nostrils puckering, as he suckled on her clit, pulling her right to the edge…and then stopping. She moaned anxiously, opening her eyes – she hadn't even actually realised that they'd been closed – only to find him kissing up her body, lips grazing her covered breasts and then teasing their way oh so slowly up her neck.

And there they lingered, nipping and kissing and suckling on her throat until her head spun, the curvaceous mare putty in his hands. They were such different hands to her paws too, which were tipped with hoof-like, chunky nails rather than small human fingertips and delicate nails, and they felt completely different on her breasts, squeezing and groping softly as he pressed into her soft flesh. Although he'd said that, well, he hadn't exactly gone all the way with anyone else either – whether furry or human – Isaac had certainly proven himself a lover willing to learn and practice the skills required to please her, something that Cherry was very much ecstatic about. It was hard to be anything but ecstatic when his mouth was between her legs but him nibbling on her neck in that way that made every muscle in her body relax, softening and turning, near enough, to goo was a close second.

Yet he needed more, her lightly muscled lover – he was going to the gym more since he'd gotten with her and it was showing, bit by bit – and his lips brushed hers, a kiss that she readily returned. Cherry's tongue, however, was the first to dare to dip between his lips and he welcomed her in, allowing her to take the lead, although the virgin mare was none the more experienced than he was.

It didn't matter, however, if they fumbled. Heaven knew they'd made enough mistakes during the course of their dating, making things work around their studies, which were, of course, still of the utmost importance despite their budding romance. A little slip or awkward moment wasn't going to unsettle either of them as long as they remembered what was truly important in the grand scheme of things. And that thing that was so very important? Cherry moaned into his mouth, losing herself in the kiss. Well, that was just the two of them, together, of course.

But, when he broke the sweet kiss, anxiety rung across his face, a tightness that was never usually present there.

"Are..." Bless him, Isaac couldn't even get a full sentence out, red in the face but not from the heat. "Are you...ready? Do you..?"

But the question did not need to be completed or even repeated as she sealed the deal with a kiss, heart hammering as it leapt in her chest. Her pussy clenched down reflexively but his hand was no longer there as he gently worked his way up her body, stroking and massaging wherever his fingers brushed: her hip, her flank, her breast. And Cherry arched into every touch, need rising as his fingers tugged the sheets away from her breasts and, so very gently, pinched a nipple.

She needed him!

The mare groaned and spread her legs for her lover, shakily wrapping them up around his hips as if to draw him down into her. But Isaac, alas, was just as sweetly inexperienced as her and, as he kissed her muzzle softly, it was as if he was trying to give himself something to do that he *knew* he could do without shaking hands or fingers that wanted to wander off elsewhere, unsure of himself in the heat of the moment. The redness of his blush, arousal hard in his hand, crept down his neck and Cherry turned his face up to hers gently, fingers curled around his cheeks.

"Hey..." She breathed. "I love you."

And maybe that was all he needed to hear as his lips twitched and broke into a goofy grin all of a sudden, his smile stretching wider and wider and wider even as he kissed her fiercely once more, crushing his lips clumsily to hers. Cherry giggled into his mouth, giddy with lust, and trembled in anticipation of what was to come.

It was as awkward as she'd always thought it would be, her lover mumbling an apology against her lips as he grasped his cock and tried to sink home. Of course, it took more than a single attempt to slip inside her but Isaac was determined, his blush warming her muzzle as he pressed in closer to her.

"Sorry... Sorry!"

But Cherry didn't need to hear apologies when everything was going just as she'd imagined. With a hushed little giggle trickling from her lips, the mare rolled her hips up against him, luck on her side. As if in a dream, his cock pressed into her soft, pussy lips, the flesh giving gently against him, and he thrust in, slipping into her wet sex in a sudden rush that was unexpectedly sharp in the taking. Inhaling quickly, the mare grabbed at his shoulders, mane stuck to her neck, damp with sweat, holding him in close in case he was thinking about pulling out any time soon.

Of course, her lover wasn't about to draw back even a single inch unless it was to thrust again, filling her completely. But he did not yet have the confidence for that and, moaning softly, quietly, he kissed her lips, a chaste kiss to go with the slow, smooth penetration as he allowed her to take the weight of his body. And Cherry wrapped her arms around him, breath catching as he eased oh so very slowly deeper, so slowly, in fact, that he must have been anxious about hurting her.

She smiled... It was sweet, really, it was, but he was by no means large enough to hurt her, although her pussy clenched and tightened pleasantly around him. Feeling his flesh penetrate her was a far cry from a dildo or even his fingers and she shuddered bodily, panting into his neck as he hilted inside her, as deep as he could possibly go.

"Ohhhh..."

Had that moan really come from her lips? She flushed heavily and shook her head but there was no taking it back, her vocalisation of pleasure, as he rocked his hips slowly, drawing back only a scant couple of inches to thrust shortly, seemingly unwilling to draw back too far. And that suited Cherry just fine as the mare whimpered and bared her throat to his shaky kisses and nibbles, head spinning as her virginity was sweetly stripped from her for the first and last time.

There was no going back.

But it was all for the better and she moaned and rocked her hips up into each and every one of his erratic, juddering thrusts, revelling in the sheer sensation of being filled. It was so much better than any toy, even though her pussy was more accepting of larger sizes than a human woman's may have been on first penetration. It did not detract from her pleasure in the slightest as her marehood squeezed and clenched reflexively around his full length, Isaac grunting as his shoulders rounded.

"Ah..." He closed his eyes, lips agape in a silent moan. "Oh... Cherry!"

It seemed that there was no time for words as he groaned and pressed his lips once more to hers, one hand coming up to tangle in her mane, drawing her in even closer to him. This time, however, he seemed to grow in confidence, taking a firmer hold on her as she swooned beneath him. Time seemed to have no meaning whatsoever for the two of them as the night darkened outside, the only light in the bedroom that of the buzzing, slightly scatty electric lamp that flickered on and off at the worst of times. It was not the most flattering of lighting but neither of the lovers were paying particular attention to the nuances and curves of each other's bodies, Isaac's muscle glaring down the lines of his back as he grunted and thrust as if his life depended on it.

Even if his life did not depend on it, perhaps his happiness did. For all Isaac wanted from his life was to spend every single last passionate moment of it with the sweet red-roan mare beneath him. Kissing her lips deeply, he groaned into her mouth and worked his glutes, driving into her with greater rhythm and passion than ever before. His body found a natural sort of pace and rhythm that made his head spin while his mare twisted beneath him, hooves digging into his buttocks as she tightened her grip on him even further.

She couldn't hold back, couldn't draw rest or respite from the tightening in her body. Every nerve ending tingled with an inner fire as Cherry nickered and whinnied wantonly, breaking the kiss as her lust got the better of her. More and more, the sensation grew, warming her from the inside out as the mare raced towards her peak like a racer on the home stretch. Panting as heavily as a racehorse herself, the mare gasped for breath that did nothing at all to alleviate the burning in her lungs as Isaac drove into her, lips at her neck and teeth nipping sharply down the line of her throat.

His hand wormed between them, thumb on her pulsing, engorged clit – and that did it. She couldn't hold back for even a moment longer and Cherry neighed surely loudly enough to disturb everyone else who may or may not have been in the dorm: what did it matter if she did? Her head spun and she reeled, dizzy in the height of the moment, wave after wave of pleasure sweeping her up and away, like the tide on that trip to the beach she'd taken with Isaac only a few weeks ago. He'd told her how strong the currents were and kept her safe between them but the current powering through her at that time had to have been far stronger than any rip that would have sought to drag her out to sea and claim her for its own.

"Fuck!"

That was Isaac but she barely noticed his crude cry as he clung to her, worming his hands around behind her back to pin her in place against him as her pussy rippled. There was no escaping the pulse and squeeze of her hot passage, juices soaking his cock and crotch with her lusty cream, and he closed his eyes tightly, his attempt to think of anything else besides simply how hot she was completely and utterly inadequate.

Like the mare, he climaxed with a start, howling nearly loudly enough to overpower her neigh, which had faded into a whickering grunt in the back of her throat as ecstasy escaped her in a rush of breath. Isaac pressed his forehead into her neck, body contorted and his pleasure only slightly muffled as he hammered into her, his thrusts beyond his control as he jerked and juddered, filling her with his cream. Each spurt of virile cum seeped deeper and deeper and, although she was on the pill (of course), he could not help but imagine just what it would be like to see her trotting around with a heavy, pregnant belly.

The thought of knocking her up, while it would have scared off other men, only made him harder and he growled breathlessly as he thrust and coaxed out every last drop of seed he had to give her, back juddering as his chest heaved for breath. It was not beyond his reach, however, even as he drew in air, leaning into his lover as he kissed her as tenderly as he was able with Cherry nuzzling into him, seeking out every bit of his face and neck that she had not kissed as yet and revisiting it in exquisite detail.

It was as perfect as any moment could have been, something purely for the two of them and ultimately no one else – not ever. For, no matter what happened in the remainder of their lives the memory would always be a sweet one that they could hold close, like each other, at the worst of times, bringing warmth to a dismal night and brightness where darkness appeared to overcome all.

It was hard, however, for Cherry to think of anything as her orgasm tapered off, the warm afterglow radiating through her as if she was immersing herself in a bath of hot water, searing her skin through her short coat in the most pleasant of ways. But everything was far more tactile and tangible than that, the fact demonstrated by the lover in her arms and his goofy smile, blinking over and over again at her as if he could not quite believe both his eyes *and* his luck.

"Isaac..." She breathed, blinking as she tried to come back to some sense of herself. "Oh, Isaac..."

How sweet was his name rolling from her lips? Cherry smiled faintly, not because she had nothing to make her smile wider but more that every drop of energy in her body seemed to have seeped away, the muscles needing to widen her smile sore from her moans and cries. It did not matter though as she ran her fingers through his hair and down his back over and over again, memorising the muscle and tone in her lover's skin as if she was never going to see him again.

Yet he would be there with her for more years than she could imagine on the loss of her virginity, the human snuggling breathlessly into the crook of her thick, mare-ish neck as he drifted away. She chuckled and let him, kissing his head and whispering sweet nothings as her ears flicked first one way and then the other, striving to catch every last nuance and lilt of his sleepy breathing.

For the moment was one that she would never again have for her own and, well, some moments were worth hanging onto, even if they would soon be gone. Where memory could fade, she would hold onto hers for dear life, clinging to her first time with all the sweetness it contained. It would always be true to her and, while it would never, ever be the very best sex she'd ever had, she could not have chosen a better partner to experience it with.

Yes... Cherry smiled, closing her eyes. She was a very lucky mare. A very lucky mare indeed.

And, as her lover slept in her arms, cock slipping from her pleasantly sore marehood, she drifted off too into her own kind of dreamland, although the blessing in their relationship was the closeness that they shared with one another.

Outside, the snow fell more heavily, thickening in the air with a flurry of urgency. There would be no going back out into the storm that night as the wind rose and howled, battering at the windows and clawing at the gutters like a wild beast of a frozen wasteland. But neither Cherry nor Isaac was awake to hear it, pressing closer as one or the other of them – they'd never quite know which – drew the bedspread over them, shielding them from the chill of the outside world.

The wind whispered, its howl dying. There was no reason for the flurry of snowflakes to do anything but dampen the sound of the world, flake by flake, the campus slowly becoming coated in a layer of white that would blanket the buildings for days to come. Somewhere, an owl hooted, ruffling its feathers against the cold. Yet even he was quiet, subdued as winter took hold while others curled into the warmth of a lover, secluded sweetly away from icy fingers.

Let the lovers lie a while longer.

Breaking Free

Gina moaned as her human lover kissed down her neck, heart fluttering and jumping wildly as if it could not simply be kept under control. The canine anthro twisted back and forth, the sheets of the bed tangled around her legs and yet, for the very first time, it did not feel like she was trapped there. Her black and white husky fur could find freedom at any time as Maverick very kindly and gently nuzzled down her neck, kissing her breasts with the utmost reverence, his touch so light that it was as if he expected her to push him away.

But the husky did not – not that time. It had happened time after time again, of course, when she'd been trying to get past everything. No one had ever told her it had been easy and yet it seemed like everyone and their dog (a little inside joke for her) expected as such. After *he'd* had his paw down between her legs, groping and teasing and shoving his fingers up into her, she'd very rightly thought that she'd never again want to be with a male, let alone a human. They were all the same, her sisters had told her, drying her tears, worry lining their features, muzzles wrinkled with shared stress for her. They only wanted one thing. They didn't realise that anthros and humans were all the same but those outside where civility came into effect, the bigger towns and cities, still thought that they should be nothing more than pets on leashes.

But Gina and the rest of anthro canine kind, walking on two legs, simply the equivalent to raw humanity, were so much more than that. Stronger and faster and, in some cases, more resilient, they could push on through where a human would have given up, their worth evident regardless of how one looked at it. She'd done so much for her family and her friends even in her younger years that they had all urged her to go off to college when the opportunity of a scholarship had presented itself and yet...the good in that remained to be seen.

Being pinned against a wall, the rank breath of a male with lank, dark hair shoved up into her face, was not what she expected of her experience in the first month. She'd begged him to stop but something primal in her had shut down, freezing with her eyes wide and strained and yet her mind pulling back and away from the scene playing out before her. There was only so much, after all, that a mind could take while a body was abused and, even after it was all said and done, her jaw aching and a foul taste in the back of her mouth, Gina could not say just what had happened in its entirety. Her clothes had been ripped, skirt beyond modest repair, and she'd limped back to her accommodation, dully, woodenly, tears streaming down her cheeks and muzzle.

Of course, the trial had been publicised and that was the end to her time at college. It had not been all that bad as the man, for once, had actually been convicted and was serving time for his crime. She hadn't been expelled from college either, of course, and had been offered the chance to complete her studies remotely, for which she was grateful, even if it took her some time to come around to the notion that she might just be worthy of doing the course and scholarship for a degree that she had gone there originally to achieve. Her family had been her rock, as hard as it was for Gina to lean on them even after everything, taking her home and into their arms once more.

The outward wounds healed. She smiled and put on a face, a mask of makeup day in and day out that was designed for husky fur and not human skin. People stopped recognising her in the street (a little dark eyeliner to change her markings did help that one along). But the touch of a man – any male, in fact – still sent her into throes of despair, spiralling down and down and down as her body and mind alike expected to relive (understandably though horrifically so for such a trauma) that terrible night all over again. She couldn't be near a male for a long time as the years passed and she completed her college course, although she did not attend the graduation ceremony where everyone, even then, recognised her name at the establishment. She learned, slowly, to stand near males again without fleeing with her tail tucked between her legs. Things came. Slowly. Too slowly.

For it was not living for her when she was scared and haggard, still a mere shell of the husky that she had been. And that was just where Maverick had come in, the man with shy eyes and a slender figure asking her out to coffee one day while she was just popping down to the store for something she'd misplaced for the evening meal she'd planned. And she'd never again find herself in such a fortunate situation as to shakily pass over her number with all the last drops of trust she had left in her very nearly dry reservoir and get to know Maverick.

He had not known about her but he was sweet and had readily held her when she'd cried, even when the nightmares returned and woke her in the dead of the night, simply because he was beside her. He'd said that he should give her space, maybe sleep on the floor, but Gina had pushed through it for him, just to see what they could have together, to give the first real relationship in her life a fair chance, a fair shot at righting all the wrongs that had come just when they were capable of causing the most damage.

They'd come through for one another and yet still one barrier to their sweet relationship remained and that was the conclusion of intimacy: full sex. Some oral had been theirs to partake in, as much as she had trembled, and yet the pleasure of coming together had encouraged Gina to try again, to keep pushing herself, little by little, to be the husky she'd always been meant to be even before that man had come into her life. For her past could not dictate her future and she refused to live a single day in that world ever again.

Heaving for breath, she panted heavily, eyes rolling and paws slipping down his back, finding the curve of his lower back and his buttocks, squeezing and teasing. It was all playful and her freedom over his body did not mean that he had freedom over hers and so she took his hand, kissed his lips and placed that hand over her breast, saying even without words that it was okay.

"Gina..."

He breathed, breath tickling her neck, and she shivered, ears slipping down, splaying gently. How did he do that to her? There was simply something about Maverick that made her feel safe and warm and content, perfect just as she was. He did everything for her that he had never been required to and she loved him dearly for that, perhaps then more than ever.

She took a deep breath, eyes strained and breasts juddering up, erratic even in the little muscle twitches of the rest of her body. She was ready. And, if she turned out not to be, it would be okay either way.

Chuckling, Maverick allowed her to roll him over onto his back, following the guiding push of her paw, the husky straddling his hips with a whimper that was meant to be seductive but really just came out as needy. His brown eyes locked with hers and he smiled warmly as he took her paw in his, although his hard, twitching shaft, complete with a slick of pre-cum, told a different tale. Maverick needed her and yet he was far too much of a gentleman to take her without asking, although a large part of that was because he valued their relationship too much. Maybe he could have tried to pressure her in their early days together but, truth be told, he wouldn't have gotten very far then before her sisters kicked him to the kerb, seeming to know when Gina was on the edge of trouble even before her instincts kicked in too. Although she did not live with them anymore, they were her protectors and defenders at all times, her greatest friends and advocates. And the fact that they thought Maverick was a good man spoke volumes about him as a person.

"Maverick..."

She whispered his name in turn, loving the way it sounded coming from her lips, rolling the sound around her mouth and breathing easier even as her chest tightened. After all, she was right there where she needed to be and, above all, she was safe. With her lover beneath her, it was finally time to take that next step.

He must have not quite believed that she was going to do it, moaning and whispering sweet things to her as she rubbed her pussy over his achingly hard shaft, the smooth, human flesh begging attention. He felt good in her mouth even though she preferred when he also had his head between her thighs at the same time, teasing the act of giving out with receiving to make it something new and different to her. But her tongue was not for his length that day and she moaned softly, rolling her head from one shoulder to the other, even though the action alone didn't do anything to release the tension and kinks found there.

Slowly, so slowly, she bore down, breath catching in her throat. His tip pressed to her entrance and then Maverick's hands were on her forearms, mumbled words flying out in a rush, stumbling over one another in their raw haste to be heard. She didn't have to do it, he said, he never wanted to force her. But it was too late to go back and it was a decision made, well and truly, for all the right reasons as the husky teased the very tip of his shaft into her pussy, her hips placed at just the right angle at just the right time. No further foreplay was needed after all the kissing and teasing, touches of lips and fingers to taunt and further the dream of what was, Gina exhaling in a rush as, very slowly still, she sank down.

No. No, she had never had that before. Not like how it was with Maverick. He sat up and held her to him, the fronts of his thighs supporting her as a base to lean back on even as she straddled him, his arms around her. He was there for her and she only had to take as much as she wanted to, although she really was a "go hard or go home" kind of husky at heart. That was one thing that he hadn't been able to strip from her.

But, although Maverick was only of average size, truly, it was harder than she'd expected to take him, sinking down and down and down until he was hilted inside her. He did not bottom out inside her – she was a little larger than him, after all, but it had never been something that really caught her attention in any way – but seated himself in there perfectly, her nose tucked into his neck as Gina's breath came in short, sharp flutters.

"Shush... I've got you..."

There was no real reason to reassure her for Gina's heart pounded with exhilaration, skin tingling and sweating lightly beneath her fur – not terribly but just enough to remind her how hot all of it was. It was never intended to be an act that her mind feared, switching into overdrive as it sought to protect her from further harm, but something to bring her pleasure and to bring her and her partner ever closer together. That knowledge in itself was power.

She kissed him then, fiercely, desperately, locking her lips with his as if it was the last kiss she would ever have, coming together sloppily and messily. An anthro canine's tongue was never designed to tease against a human's but they managed well enough, regardless of the excess saliva. A sloppy kiss truly was by the by as his cock, after all, hilted inside her, Gina sitting down on his length to squeeze and ripple around him, that familiar tightening coming with fresh lilts in the pit of her belly. Did her body really want to orgasm – already?

Her heart pounded and she rocked against him, grinding her clit lightly through the curl of pubic hair at his crotch, enough stimulation to have her panting and gasping on the very edge of climax. And her partner knew her and her body well enough by then to know how close she was, kissing her even more deeply than he already was as she plunged her tongue into his mouth, curling up against his. Grazing through the soft fluff around her pussy, he found her clit, even as he trembled, and circled it, pressing down sweetly and stimulating it in all the ways that he knew got her going, her hips bucking frantically until that moment that they'd both lusted after came.

She climaxed on his cock. With a howl, her head flew back in a cheeky spray of spittle (they'd giggle about that one later, however red their cheeks were) and she bucked and humped, thrusting herself unknowingly on his shaft, mimicking sex. And it had been so very long for Maverick too that he hunched forward, arms tight around his lover to hold her close and protect her, to keep her close from the nuance of any harm at all that may come her way. He was there for her and she for him, two hearts pounding together as her pussy rippled and pulled at his shaft.

He exhaled in a rush of breath into her shoulder even as she climaxed, the hump and grind of her body impossible to ignore. And yet he did all he could to hold back, Gina's head spinning and spinning as his fingers tightened, digging into muscle and softer flesh even through her thicker layer of fur. She still needed to shed but that was by the by as he gritted his teeth, cock throbbing and pulsing. Gina could not quite feel that even with his length crammed up into her, desperate for release, but her orgasm dying down did give her the courage and the strength to rock her hips with more determination and poise, lifting herself a little as her breasts squashed against his chest.

"Maverick," she breathed, a giggle on her lips. "Oh... That was so quick... Are you...?"

A question did not always need an answer, however, and his lips on hers sealed the deal as she excitedly whined into the kiss, heart in her mouth. Oh, how her body and her mind needed him, although she already had climaxed, the emotional connection there in spades, as much as she ever could have wished for. Moaning, she squeezed him close, relishing in every last sensation as she murmured for him to fill her, to seed her full. Unlike that time when she had been dragged out into the alleyway with tears in her eyes, she had a lover there she could trust and rely on, one who put her pleasure before his and had, above all else, *waited* for her to be ready for him. And that was just why she needed the ultimate gift from him, his throbbing cock drooling pre-cum even as he pumped and grunted with a masculine air that sent a cool shiver down the husky's spine. Still, it did not dampen her lusts in the slightest.

Neither of them considered the fact that, well, Maverick's shaft was unwrapped. Yet a pup out of their sweet liaison could only have made things all the better, even though that fact remained to be seen in the coming months. Not many huskies like her, after all, took their first time and they were willing to keep trying for the little one that they yearned to bring into the world.

If it was right for them, that was.

Closer and closer, she ground on him and panted heavily, desire tightening once again in the prelude to a blissful orgasm, need coursing through her with each and every stroke. It was clumsy and a little erratic, her first real time, but it was all that she could ever have asked it to be, her lover pressing up harder against her in those heated moments before the dam burst. And yet it could not all last forever, as much as she suddenly wanted it to, climaxing together in a howl and a moan, a furred body and a masculine one grinding and rocking together as his cock spurting, delivering the dose of seed to her that she craved.

They kissed, moaning and groaning lightly through orgasm, her ears slipped back in lust. And yet they too had to slow down, to come down from the pinnacle of an event that had ended up all too brief. Yet Gina would have many more times, even if they would never again match up to her very first time, with her lover, their bodies coming together as they entwined their fingers and whispered their wants and needs late into the night. There was plenty of time left for the two of them to satisfy those wants and needs too, lusting after and coming together time after time again for the bliss that sexual liaisons could provide.

It was never meant to be a dark time, only light. And Maverick opened that door for Gina, leading her through with a smile on his face and her arm tucked into his, as safe and secure as she ever could be with him. Yet the knowledge of one thing remained to glow out the darkness, light shining through to spear the shreds of black as if they had never had any place in her heart and soul to begin with.

The husky smiled.

Her first time was always the one that she would love the most.

Finally

"I'm so glad…that we don't have to worry about that ever again…"

The naga curled around his partner, the tip of his rattlesnake-like tail flicking back and forth with a light, typical rattle. Of course, Lei was not a rattlesnake, not with having an anthro, humanoid-like torso clad in brown and tan and cream python scales, but he was his own kind of naga through and through. They didn't have to follow typical types of snakes, of course, when they were their own species, breaking norms and finding love, just like all the other anthros in the world.

Though he could not have been more grateful to be there with his partner, Becky, secluded away in the treehouse dwelling: a much-needed holiday for them. Of course, the treehouse was more of a natural environment for the anthro blue macaw, yellow flashes on her wing feathers and a darker streak in her tail, but he was happy to be up there too. The abode was pleasant with a solid staircase up to it, big and spacious with the boughs of the tree built through the holiday home. It would have been more of a fancy or lure to those that were not used to accommodations like that, but, honestly, Lei could not have found something more appropriate for Becky and him, especially after such a trying time.

Becky would always have a bare patch of feathers on her chest where…it had been removed, all the surgeries, and another on her arm where the IV drip had gone in. Apparently, too much trauma to the skin could cause the feathers to simply not grow back and Becky had been in hospital for quite some time.

The naga's black tongue flickered in and out of his muzzle and he shook his head, laying his love back gently on the bed, low and set into the floor of the open plan living and sleeping area. Birds called outside, native species to the area, but Lei was not concerned about that anymore.

Not when he had his Becky back, his beautiful macaw, in his arms. And that was where she would stay, forevermore.

"Hey... It's okay, darling," she murmured, giving him a light, pecking kiss on the side of his snout. "Everything's okay. We don't have to think about any of that right now, I've got the "all clear," it's been three years now... Let's just enjoy this."

Lei murmured his agreement, the naga sliding down her body with a more mischievous smile on his lips than before. For there was one way, most certainly, that the naga could think of to take their minds off things, for that was exactly what their holiday was supposed to be for.

Reconnecting. Loving. Spending time with each other, however they pleased.

And her bare, blue feathers beckoned him as he spread her naked form out on the bed like a treat to be devoured, his coils shifting to push the sheets back. They would only get in the way as his tail rattled and he nuzzled adoringly at her lower stomach, at the slight softness there, though he loved it. He wanted to see her fit and strong and healthy and the sight of the thin, frail bird from all those terrible months was not something that Lei wanted to return to at all.

No... He would be there with her, his tongue flicking out between her thighs, tasting her essence. She was wet already, but that could have been due to the close proximity of his body in the bed alone, how his coils had been softly moving and wrapping around her, at least three times the length of his torso. But Becky had clearly not minded that as he curled them around her again, gently using his own coils to lift her buttocks gently for him, fanning out her tail feathers beautiful. That said, Lei would have thought that any presentation of Becky's body was beautiful.

"Oh… Lei…"

He loved the sound of his name on her lips, however wispy and faint her voice was. The macaw always struggled to enunciate her words when her breath was catching, heartbeat fluttering in her delicate ribcage, though the naga had to remember that he was the only one in the world for her that could do that, for her. It was an honour that he took well in hand and he spread her thighs even more hungrily, seeking out the treat of her pussy.

The moment was for them and them alone, even as his shaft slipped out of the slit where it was normally contained. No… Lei wasn't going to worry about his own pleasure – at least, not until Becky clucked and clicked and fluttered to make him share her pleasure too. That would come, only because his partner didn't want him to go without either, but his tongue flickered up against the damp feathers framing her pussy lips with due intent.

He knew every corner of her body, how to work the bird up slowly, but there was no need for that, not that night. Not with the stars shining high in the sky above and the moon hanging softly, bearing witness, through the open window, to their seductive tryst. Two loves coming together again, for they had spent too much time worrying and waiting, not sure where to go next, what to do, if there was still more to be had.

And, now, there was no care to be concerned about any of that for even a moment longer, not as his tongue dipped inside her, plundering her pussy, the macaw bucking her hips, digging her taloned feet down into the bed. She moaned for him and he followed the cues of her body, dragging his long, slippery tongue back up inside her, lapping again and again.

"Ah... Lei!"

She squeezed her legs around him, talons scraping against his scales, though it would take the naga a lot more than merely that to be hurt in the slightest. No, he was fine, more than fine, as long as Becky was there with him, his heart pounding more and more vibrantly. In a way, it was as if the naga was waking up again after a long period of being asleep, slumbering, watching, waiting, though it was now time to be bright again and to accept the light of day.

His bird... His pretty bird... She was beautiful inside and out and, yet again, the naga yearned to show her that, slurping up inside her with a softly lewd sound. She squeaked, trembling against him, her hands coming down with the feathers that made up her "wings" tenderly brushing the sides of his snout, around to the back of his head. She didn't have wings on her back, not like some avians, but her wings doubled as arms, with long feathers still draped from them. Unfortunately for the macaw, she could not fly, though that was quite common too.

Lei exhaled softly, nostrils fluttering, nuzzling briefly into her feathers, though he could not forget nor deny himself the treat of her pussy for any longer than needed. He dove back into the treat of her sex with a hungry growl, letting the scent of her envelop him, dragging him blissfully under.

For there was nowhere else that he would rather be than right where he was in that moment, quivering, whimpering, moaning, making all manner of noises that a naga, quite, might not have been expected to. But there was something about Becky that brought out that side of him against all the odds, shuddering into her touch, the soft tickle of her feathers pulling and picking around his face and neck, even down to his shoulders and lower still.

"Ah... Sweetie... Lei, you're too good to me..."

He wanted to be better for her, but it was hard for the naga to say that out loud while his tongue was inside her, thrusting back and forth, dragging back up and out and over the nub of her clit. He had always considered himself exceedingly fortunate that the macaw's clit was as large and as prominent as it was, for it meant that it was even easier for him to devote attention to it, to pleasure her.

And he needed that too, to feel her tensing and bucking, that high of orgasm growing closer and closer as he twirled his tongue around the nub of passion. Becky's breath hitched in her chest and the naga used the moment to his advantage as he pressed two fingers into her pussy, the taste of her lingering in his mouth. His tongue was better suited to teasing around her clit, lapping back and forth, even rapidly flicking the tip against it rapidly, bringing her to a heaving, steeping rise of pleasure.

"Ah! Lei!"

Oh, he knew that she was getting close, so close, but she still needed more, even more, to be pushed over the edge. And it was all up to him to do it, to show his love for her in one more way as he worked his fingers back and forth, curling them up inside her to hit her G-spot lightly with every stroke. Lei did not have to be all that delicate in his passion as he thrust, not when he pulled over her G-spot with every push of his hand, the macaw thrusting and grinding weakly up against him. Not that Becky needed to do anything to gain her pleasure, panting heavily, not when Lei was there to give her everything that she could have craved and more.

The macaw could not speak anymore, the edges of her beak lightly clacking as passion overwhelmed her, coursing through, his lips finally sealing carefully around her clit. He sucked it luxuriously into her mouth, lashing it with his tongue, yet the naga was still gentle with her, even as he pressed on to bring her that high. He could not hold off forever, after all, not when passion needed to be had, not when his glorious sweetheart was thrusting and rocking against him, panting through the nares on her beak.

Everything had to come through, yes, as he pressed her closer and closer, her pussy wet, so very wet and slick, around him. Her sex gripped his fingers and he knew that he was close to bringing her off into delirium, so very close, her sex rippling and pulsing – and then she was there.

She cried out, a shriek of a macaw cutting through the air, though neither of them had to worry about disturbing anyone else at all, oh no. They had the whole place to themselves and all the privacy that they could ever have wanted as he suckled on her clit, giving her due reverence and passion through the flick of his tongue and the drive of his fingers. He curled them up inside her as she ground down onto his fingers even more, passion overcoming her, but Lei was right there to help the macaw ride out the racing high of climax, hips juddering and grinding down at him with untamed and untold desire.

His tongue, however, could not help but slip down against her sex, where her juices drooled out around his fingers, for it was not all that tight of a fit with only two fingers inside her. It was just what she needed, just what was desired to bring her over the edge, to break that tension sweetly.

And they needed to be close too, as Lei nuzzled into her inner thighs, giving her a break and a rest as he exhaled softly against her feathers. Soon, the avian would be more than ready for another round and he would be ready to bring her off again, letting his body wind and lovingly twist around her so that the macaw did not have to do anything at all.

Well... Becky would do something, of course. She would not be kept down and she would not be bested, scolding him from trying to do everything for her. that was just one more thing that the naga loved about her.

Finally, they could just be together. Finally, they could put the past behind them.

Together, it was time to move forward.

Purity Bound

"My sweet... Let me show you."

Marie shivered, the white-furred bunny spread-eagled on the bed, her wrists and ankles bound to the bed-posts with purple, silk ties. That they were not proper bondage equipment did not take anything from her experience, breath catching her in throat, breasts rising as her tiny chest rose and fell, shuddering to take in the breath that she needed. Yet her body no longer seemed to be her own as her blonde hair splayed out across the pillows and her ears like a halo, the pure black stallion standing over her with a quietly dominating air, fingers clasped around the handle of something that she would soon become very familiar with.

It was not one's traditional love-story but, well...it was their love story and it was the story that Marie would tell, one day in the future, to their kids – leaving out the eroticism, of course, for that was for no one's eyes or ears than their own. Bunny meets horse, bunny falls in love with horse: happily ever after, right? Things were not as easy as that, however, with Marie being a college freshman and the studly stallion one of her tutors, a little grey around the edges and not quite as well-groomed as the younger stallions that were perhaps a little too wrapped up in how they presented themselves to the ladies (or the colts, if that was the way they swung).

Alexander had taken her heart and things had developed from there, keeping their relationship on the down-low, although, thankfully, he worked in a different department to the course of Marie's study. It didn't matter to her that he was twenty years her senior, despite the sidelong looks and comments that they got, on occasion. As far as Marie was concerned, love was love and all she needed to feel whole was the firm hold of his paw around hers.

Or on her shoulder, guiding her. On her chest, squeezing her breast. Even the smallest shift of his body had her standing to attention, excitement coursing through her that even overruled the nervousness of being in her first relationship ever.

Neither had she lost her virginity but, well...that was just what she was there to explore that night with Alexander, her sweet love and, maybe forevermore, the dominant of her heart and soul too. It was all up for grabs in the art and arms of devout experimentation. And who was to say just how things would end up for her after that night?

Alexander rubbed his chin, the hair there a little thicker as if he was growing a beard, although he most often kept himself neatly trimmed around the face, even down to the cute tufts of hair poking out of his ears. He may have been jet black with thick feather around his fetlocks but the grey hairs could not be hidden without an extensive dye job, betraying his age even though he was middle-aged only, wizened and aware of the darkness in the world while he brought his own brand of joys and pleasures into it.

Marie liked it. She said that it brought him dignity as she kissed his lips, made him seem distinguished and refined, like everyone who was in his presence should have been looking up to him. That was one of many things that she said that made Alexander blush but there was no blushing to be had from the horse as he stood over his hopelessly bound submissive, admiring the purity of her virgin body as even the light pink of her pussy was on show. His ears pricked and he huffed softly, nostrils flaring in a snort that had a shiver racing through her, a thicker muff, almost, of fur around Marie's neck where the dewlap remained of her ancestral bunny heritage.

It was adorable. Tightening his fingers around the massage wand, switched off for the moment, Alexander approached the bed with his head held high, his stride smooth and casual. Of course, he did not need to wear any clothes when his sweet submissive was as nude as the day she'd been born, his soft sheath on show while his cock plumped it out, though it would be a devout length for her to take for her first time.

But he could help with that. Very easily so.

Marie squirmed on the bed as he towered over her, an ominous and yet comforting presence at the same time. Where he excited her he protected her too, the comfort of his bulk blocking out the hate and aggression of the world, giving her a safe place, at long last even in her young years, to express herself. It didn't matter what was going on, the politics abounding within her college and the twisted truths that often only came to light after a friendship had crumbled, so many things that made her heart ache... No, none of that mattered as long as he was there with her, making her heart pound so desperately, squirming in her bondage, revelling in how exposed she was right there for him.

"Oh..."

She couldn't help herself, letting out the softest moan that had ever passed the barrier of her lips as she laid there, his paw tracing a path down between her breasts. Marie still did not recognise what he held in his other paw but, really, did it matter one bit when she had so much left to experience? He was in control and not her and the control of that gave up her freedom in the best of ways, allowing her freedom at the same time. It didn't make sense to her but there was not much in the world that could have made sense to her as his lips closed, oh so very softly and tenderly, around her breast, tugging her nipple lightly out from the paleness of the pink flesh under her fur.

She was so sweet, so innocent, and Alexander would have been a liar indeed if he did not say that that was the reason he had been so drawn to her in the first place. It was wrong and it was right and he didn't want to think about that when she was naked before him, the taste of her pussy from earlier in their session lingering on his lips, although he had not yet allowed her to orgasm.

That was what the massage wand was for.

"I think you've been a very naughty bunny," he murmured, his usually rough voice as smooth as silk as his hooves shifted on the carpet of his bedroom floor. "But I don't have punishments in store for princesses like you..."

Her heart flipped over. Oh, how he did that to her...

"But I do have rewards that may feel like that."

Her ears perked up but it was too late for Marie to do anything but moan as the wand brushed the flushed lips of her pussy, her clit pushing out very softly from the hood of flesh that usually kept it concealed. Her body was primed and ready but she was not ready in herself for the buzz of the massager as it pressed wantonly up to her sex, coaxing a cry from her. That was the end of any control that she may have thought she had over herself right then and there, hips rising and falling, bucking wantonly, a slave to the will of her body while her master controlled it for her.

Was he her master? Marie's head swam. She'd never called Alexander that, the older stallion, but it felt right, it felt natural, it felt like something that she wanted to do for the rest of her life with him. Yet there was no time to think about that as her toes curled and flexed, large hind paws jigging, wanting to free herself from the bondage just to be free to writhe and twist and express her pleasure in the most bodily of ways possible.

That was not to be, however – not as Alexander leaned over her, his cock slowly plumping out his sheath more and more. It demanded attention and some part of her, even then, wanted to reach out to it, to feel the weight of him in her comparatively tiny paw, her fingers not even closing completely around his thick girth.

Marie shivered, head swirling, swimming, pleasure clamouring for precedence as the buzz of the wand filled the bedroom, pulling at her attention. Just how was she going to take him when he was that big, however much she wanted it? But that in itself was not a decision that was for her to make – or one that she had already made, depending on how one looked at it. All she knew was that her heart pounded so desperately for him that she would have done everything he wanted and more as he teased her with the wand, bringing her to the edge from which she thought, toes curling, there could be no coming back from.

And then it faded, leaving her humping and gasping as the wand moved away, her dominant chuckling softly in the back of his throat as he rubbed his chin, eyes dancing with lightly commanding mischief.

"You didn't think it would be that easy now...did you, darling?"

He called her "darling" but it felt like something far cruder, putting her on her knees before him, less than him and yet everything too that she may have ever wanted to be. Alexander smirked, his lips quirking up only faintly, but it was still there.

The stallion snorted, cock plumping up thick and fast, swelling with blood in a smooth, black spire, skin smoothing out where the wrinkles had been present when he was soft. Yet his shaft was not quite yet destined to be used as he teased his sweetheart, so very easily commanding her body so that she could feel the rise of joys unlike anything else ever before. Of course, he'd had his muzzle between her legs before but he'd always gone at the pace of his partners, for there was no better way to dominate, letting them come to that submission under his firm paw as time came to pass. Where there was force and pushing, well, that did not bode well for longevity and Alexander wanted to have Marie with him...

He swallowed hard. Forever. Forever would have been too short but, if she'd have him, that was the deal that he'd have to take.

She whimpered and begged and he ran the wand around her breasts and nipples, showing her the electric tenacity of her body, everything that it could do for her, need thrumming through. Yet he was not about to let her get off too quickly as he teased it down and pressed it to her folds all over again, pushing it down, varying the pressure, the vibrations of the wand trembling through her with false promises.

For he was not going to let her get off that time and not even the time after that, not as she tugged helplessly at her bondage, the silk slipping around her wrists as she tried to fling herself about the bed. Yet Alexander had her fixed down so firmly that there was simply no hope of her going anywhere as he forced her to the edge again and again, pussy slick and ready and yet not brought to that dream of sweet completion. Once again, she was reminded how, willingly, she was but a toy for him, bucking and arching, even trying to make her body look as appealing as possible, something to tempt him to give her what she so very desperately needed.

Alexander was a seasoned hand at what he did, however, one paw on his cock, massaging and stroking his length slowly, patiently. Great, fat globs of pre-cum oozed from the meaty tip, flat and ready to spill forth, yet that was a very special treat for his bunny submissive, only when she was ready for it and whimpering and begging in just the right tone. His pleasure, still, was not to be denied to himself in the meantime and he watched with a heady throb of pleasure each time how her eyes flicked to his cock, wanting the beast, wanting the meat of him, her tiny, virgin body aching for something that only he could give.

She wouldn't be a virgin for much longer, however, not as he brought her too close to the edge, bearing down on her clit so that she was forced to experience the greatest pressure of the vibrations. Marie screamed yet the orgasm she expected did not come as he let her simmer down all over again, whimpering and begging, hanging there with her ears flopping as if even that part of her was not something that she could control for a moment longer.

"P-please..." She whimpered, licking her lips, though there was no moisture left in her mouth, body tight with restrained desire. "Please... Let me... Can I... M-m-may I..."

Yet Marie could not even find the words with which to convey the depth of her need, reduced to a blubbering, lustful mess, licking her lips over and over again, panting harshly. Her breasts, a pleasant handful each for a large stallion like Alexander, tugged gently to either side of her chest by the will of gravity, nipples always remaining softly perky and pink, protruding through her light, silken fur.

"Are you ready?" He murmured, eyes glinting. "I have what you need, little one, if you are."

The undertone of desire could not be denied in his words as she panted and heaved, a squeal on her lips as the wand tickled her pussy once more. Blood pounded against her eardrums, the beat of her heart something that could not be hidden, pulsing through almost audibly as she needed it, needed him, her cunny as slick and as ready as she could have ever have hoped it to be.

"Yes..."

She wasn't sure if she'd actually said that word out loud but she must have done so, for the stallion's eyes crinkled at the corners, a smile reaching them that not even his dominant aura could have reached. It was time and it was the perfect time as he set the wand aside, though she hoped, with a delicious little shiver that she did not even want to control, that he would use it again that night, wanting to do more even then. She didn't know how much her first time would take out of her but, well, she would soon come to see that that stamina would both come and grow in time.

Alexander's heart pounded for the perfect beauty splayed out on the bed for his attention, helpless and arching up for his whim and his touch. His body moved fluidly over her, muscles tensing, the bed bowing lightly under the weight of his body, although it was good enough quality to not jostle his lover too badly. Nothing but the best for him but, well, he had not told Marie that he'd bought a new mattress a few months back in the hopes that she would lie there with him one day, although not even the stallion could have predicted just how wonderful she could have felt in his arms.

Their lives were intertwined forever as his cock throbbed for her, patiently drooling a touch of pre-cum over her leg as he knelt between her spread thighs, aching for her, need pounding through, desire curling to the surface. It was needed, so very much so, yet time and patience was key in bringing them together, making her first time one that she would remember forever for all the right reasons, though he had to be mindful too of the size of his shaft.

Marie wasn't thinking of that, however, trying to reach him even as his chest gently pressed down to her. The bunny's soft body arched up to meet him, lips parted, his own pressed to hers, tongue dominating her mouth. The fleshy swathe of his tongue teased against hers, lapping and twining, yet Marie could not have hoped to match up to him and all his experience, the disparity between them as exciting as it was nerve-wracking.

Please...

With his mouth covering hers, dominating her with a kiss, she could not beg him for what they both wanted, though the thickness of his shaft lying against her thigh denoted exactly what she wanted right there and then. She'd already voiced her consent and he knew it too, ears flicking to the tenor of her moans, needing more, wanting more, the two of them hungry for the crux of desire unlike anything that they had ever come across. It was new, even to Alexander, though he was still able to break the kiss and slow everything down a notch as he breathed a little more rapidly, love shining in his eyes for her.

"I love you, little one."

Yet Marie could not reply as he positioned the flat tip of his cock against her pussy, her legs trying to spread more, whimpering his name in a broken bubble of breath. Oh, she needed him, needed him so very badly, so lost in desire that she wanted to do everything for him right there and then even though he had bound her to take that need strictly away from her. With his cock in one paw, hoof-like fingertips tenderly cupping around, Alexander snorted softly yet did not hold back from slipping into her, her pussy reluctant to yield for a heartbeat of a moment that seemed to stretch on forever as she held her breath.

And then it was in, slipping forth in a thrust of flesh as if it had been released from a spring, her entrance giving way as her folds stretched around him, welcoming him in, teasing him deeper. Her breath caught at how large he was but he had teased her for so long already that she was slick enough to take him, stretching her out wonderfully without an ounce of pain, just as it was meant to be. Taking her cherry, after all, didn't have to hurt and she moaned loudly, turning the side of her face into the pillow, nose twitching faintly, lost in sensation as he filled her more and more, slipping deeper and deeper.

It was all he could do to take it slowly for her, opening her up and allowing her folds to ripple around him, her body striving to respond even as he asked that it take the largest shaft she had to date – even from her small collection of sex toys! It was a big ask for her and, even as her dominant in the moment, he had to be respectful of that, the bunny a good two feet shorter than him even then, her body small and petite and not designed for a cock like his.

Still, she wanted it, panting hungrily, her teeth showing, though they did not hold the threat in them that a predator may have. Her ears flicked forward as if springing to attention and he drew back at just the right moment to control her, grinding in with a short, sharp thrust as he sent her spiralling into her very first orgasm on his cock.

Humping and twisting, Marie was barely aware of the stallion pinning her in place, his hand-like "paws" (the terms were interchangeable for their concerns) needed in addition to the bondage to prevent her from hurting herself, muscles bunching as he put his weight into holding her. All she knew was pleasure: great, ferocious, crashing waves of pleasure, sweeping through her, setting fire to her veins and letting the wildness of it flow through her. Her body was not her own but it was owned by one who would care for it with all his heart and keep her close to his heart at all times, hips rocking and bucking, grinding her strained pussy down even further on her cock before she was strictly ready for it.

The stallion grunted and thrust, letting her dictate, if only for a short while, just how much of his cock she would take, riding her out through her orgasm. The rippling of her pussy, while erratic, was difficult to resist even for a stallion like him, hardly in the business of spending his load quickly, thrusting smoothly and seamlessly. After all, he had many years of experience behind him as he thoroughly deflowered the virgin. He took her purity so sweetly that she may not have even been aware that she'd lost it if not for the bulge of his cock showing, very lightly and faintly, through her abdomen, needing space to go as her tiny body made way for it.

He had his needs too even as she moaned and panted, lips forming his name over and over again, his cock disappearing into the hungry flower of her pussy. She closed around him and he held one of her paws as if to pin it away, although the silk tie already kept it right where it needed to be, her body arching up to meet each and every one of his thrusts, finding a rhythm despite the ache running through her. For that was, perhaps, what sex and lovemaking was all about, finding the rhythm of a partner and pushing through for sweet exultation.

Marie's head rolled back against the pillows, her lover's lips on her neck, body straining, aching, pulling at her bondage – not because she wanted to get away from him by any means but simply because she wanted to experience everything to its fullest. What the bunny, however, did not yet know was that she had to let things happen to experience them as they were, not jumping from one thing to another, giving her body over to the will of another. That was just what her grunting dominant of a stallion was there for, however, his thrusts growing in power and force as he spread her open around him, moaning out loud.

"Fuck, bunny..."

She shivered. It was better when he didn't use her name. She'd have to tell him that later.

Alexander was too lost in the moment though to consider the finer details, tremors of control tingling through him as his bunny shuddered. She must have already been building to another orgasm from how she squeezed down around his shaft, managing to bury his cock in past the thickness of the medial ring, marvelling breathlessly at just how much she was able to take. Maybe it was just how her body was or maybe it was something else, something more, something that made her want to please him above all else, everyone else, in the whole wide world.

It didn't matter though as long as she was with him, one last virginity of hers left to take in her feminine sex, for he was yet to spend his seed inside her, claiming her completely. It was the ultimate mark, to let another mount one bareback and take their cum, and that was just what he planned to do. Snorting heavily, his tail swished in a raspy flick of hair, Marie's breath catching beneath him, dark eyes fixed on him as she stared up at him in complete and utter adoration. With a heady groan that rose from the back of his throat, not even sounding like him, he knew with a settled sensation of belonging that that was just how he looked at her too.

He tightened his grip on her paw as he powered into her, bolder than ever as her pussy swallowed up every one of his thrusts. He was able to put more force behind them, even though he was not using his full strength, but it was a taste of the dominance he could offer her as the silk ties pulled tight, Marie teetering on the edge of another climax.

Yet it was that climax that he would tie in with his own as he nipped at her neck, leaving his mark on her with a wash of warm breath, the bunny's cries filling the bedroom as she spiralled into orgasm. It was not for her to control but it was for the stallion to ride her out through it all over again, scooping a paw under her buttocks to lift her up to his cock as he sought to cram another inch or two inside her, testing her limits, while the tip of his cock pressed up to her innermost barrier. It was hard to do at the height of such desire but he could angle it just right to get up alongside that barrier, a softer span of flesh allowing that seductive true penetration, his cock pulsing, grinding, aching for release.

Marie would have clung to him if she could have but the moment was his to take her through just as she pleased, heart hammering in the bliss of losing control, rocking and trembling, though she wasn't really moving very much at all. She didn't have to in order to submit to him, the stallion of her life, his cock disappearing into her hot, wet tunnel as her folds closed around him, sloppy and lewd with her soaked arousal. Her pussy tried to squeeze down on him but that climax was for the two of them as his balls just about managed to bounce off her cunny, a whinny heralding a release of a higher pleasure.

And then Alexander lost all control as he emptied his balls into her, lost in the moment yet still in control, grunting and snorting, huffing like a wild stallion as he powered into her. He demanded that her pussy suck down every inch of his cock that he was willing to give, the extra depth allowing his cock-tip to flare out, spending spurt after spurt deep up inside her. His thrusts forced his cum out along the length of his cock even as he thrust but that was not about to stop him as Marie's toes curled and flexed, crying out as her orgasm pounded through her.

He wouldn't stop, taking her completely and utterly, her body willingly his to do with as he commanded, although he was respectful of the limits her body presented to him. It didn't stop him from enjoying the slick sheen on the part of his cock lingering outside her pussy, staying as deep as possible to pound into her, letting her milk him and milk him even though Marie could not have been aware of what her body was doing even then.

The orgasm may have been the pinnacle but there was a softening to come, his paws gently untying her bondage, staying inside her for as long as possible even as his cock softened, teasing and easing from her as much as he strove to linger. Marie moaned, head rolling from one shoulder to the other, every last bit of her vitality and energy stripped from her in those multiple orgasms, stamina coveted but leaving much to be desired. She would get there though, her want and need leading her to kneel before him each and every night as she learned what it was to be his submissive, Marie leading while he allowed her that submissive freedom of true expression.

She was in his arms for a long time, cradled there, recovering, relaxing in the afterglow and slowly coming back to some sense of herself, her control over her body returning. It was sweetening and softening but he needed to rise at some point, kissing her forehead and standing. Stretching out his arms over his head, Alexander caught her looking, casting her a sly glance back over his shoulder, though Marie was not swift enough to act like she was still drowsy, a faint blush prickling to life in her cheeks and warming the interiors of her ears.

The stallion's cock twitched, flushing faintly with blood all over again, and Marie gasped, eyes wide.

He wanted her. She swallowed. Could she ever have wanted anything more?

"Come here."

Pointing to the rug, he snapped his fingers, an eyebrow raised as if merely waiting for her to get into position. Even though her body ached pleasantly from her very first time, something that would be softly and sweetly relived between the two of them over wine and entrees later on, she wanted something more, something that she had never even the once considered before Alexander came into her life.

For all she needed was to be at his hooves above all else, her head bowed and ears trembling up as she prostrated herself before him, letting him know, well and truly, that he was the dominant of her soul, her heart and everything she was. Her hair fell down her neck in a mostly sheer fall, a little mussed where she had tossed and writhed on the bed, though Alexander's fingers combed it out as his cock rose swiftly back to full hardness as if it had never softened at all. He was a stud and a breeder too at that, everything that she could have ever have wanted in a partner as he drew her head back slowly, smiling as he rubbed his cock against her face.

Marie whimpered, pussy dampening softly, her folds clenching even though her cunny could not hope to keep the slickness of his seed in there with how much he had stretched her. She was right where she wanted to be and the rest of her life with Alexander, her lover forever, had opened up before her like the petals of a rare flower.

Was she that flower? She felt like it sometimes, what with how he looked at her. Yet he had his cock pressed to her muzzle, an eyebrow raised, forelock flopping across his other eye in a way that, strangely, made her heart turn over. She'd have a lot more of that in the future, after he collared her and made her his forever.

Alexander nickered, tail flicking, drawing her attention back to him, the throbbing of his cock, glistening faintly with a combination of his seed and her sweet arousal. Her mouth moistened.

"You have work to do, little one."

Marie licked her lips, ears slipping back submissively.

"What would you have me do, master?"

Alexander's nostrils twitched as he smirked, eyes alight with dark desire that he had not had the chance to let out to play in so very long.

It was as if she didn't have to ask...

Eaten Out on a Work Call

"Yes, I heard about that. What I think we should do about the dropping sales is…"

Melanie's eyelids drooped, though the feline anthro didn't feel as if she was in any position to be falling asleep, not when there was so much going on in her company. In accounts rather than the sales team, she didn't understand why she'd had to be present remotely on the work meeting anyway, half of the office on site and half remote still. "Koom" call system had exploded while they'd been forced to be away from the office, even though the cat wasn't exactly all that sure that she enjoyed the system. There were only so many times, after all, that she could ask if someone could hear her or not, doubting her rather spotty internet connection.

Still, sales or bad sales were a concern and one that set her gut rumbling with discontent, wondering if the rather large meatball sub that she had devoured for lunch had been all that much of a good idea or not. Sat upon the uncomfortable chair in her home office, the guest bed was only just out of sight behind her, though she was glad, at least, that she had remembered to make it up again after her last guest had left. It had only been her brother, of course, visiting for the weekend, but the tabby cat could be a right slob when he wanted to be. Which, around her, was pretty much all the time, still expecting his big sister in her twenties to pick up after him. Still, she loved him as much as she seethed at him.

Melanie was the perfect likeness to her brother and she imagined that she bore the same bored expression on her face as she sat there, appearing attentive with some slight nods and general sounds of affirmation, just to show that she was listening. Her silver tabby coat gleamed with good health, though she had applied a little fur oil to her face just to make sure it looked bright enough for her work laptop's webcam. She didn't usually wear make-up, least of all when she was home, and loathed even that much and the tiny flicker of mascara and eyeliner she used to brighten up her eyes too. Everyone said she looked so tired on camera, but it wasn't her fault that the lighting in the spare bedroom (AKA the office) was terrible.

They droned on and on about sales tactics and all manner of things while she pretended to be attentive, still wondering all the while just what it was that she was supposed to be paying attention to. Sure, it was worrying, but maybe they wanted someone from every department there, for she couldn't think of any other reason for her to be there. The calls were annoying, as if they were making up reasons to get them all together, perhaps even just trying to make sure that everyone there was actually working.

Who knew, ultimately? Either way, she had to show her face, nodding and tapping away on her laptop to keep herself both awake and entertained, at least to the best of her ability. Sometimes, she could only do what she could do right there and then.

The bedroom door creaked and she glanced back, luckily with her microphone on mute. She had a big set of over the ear gaming headphones that worked far better with the laptop than the built-in speaker, though Mel was still at a loss as to how she kept damaging those damn things, over and over again. She was a pro at it.

She made a sharp, sideways, cutting motion with her hand as her tortoiseshell feline boyfriend poked his head around the door, green eyes alight and his whiskers appearing to quiver. That was never a good look on him, not even when she was on his side and on board with whatever it was that he had in mind.

Go away, she mouthed, trying to get him to get the hint, without also making it look like she was "talking on the call" too much, her paw covering her mouth. *I'm busy. Love you!*

Sam, however, didn't get the hint. See, the cat had something in mind, something a little devious, and, well, he was bored on his time off from work, due to a scheduled shutdown. He'd be back soon in a week, but Mel didn't realise just how far the depths of his debauchery and need had gone. Things could come to light, of course, in boredom that never before had to be paid due attention to, though she was about to see that in the most intimate of ways...

Her boyfriend was careful, even as she kept an eye on him out of the corner of her eye, her tail flicking back and forth anxiously behind her chair, hanging down low. The old computer chair was aged enough that the squeak that emanated from somewhere near the base could not simply be oiled way and there was no manner of fixing that could update or modernise it. All Melanie could do was wince and squirm, looking down without looking like she was looking down, at least on camera.

What on earth was Sam doing? It didn't make sense, not at all, not while her boyfriend was crawling around on the floor, a smirk on his lips that didn't quite fit there. If Melanie had been focusing on her work call a little more intently, she might have been able to wedge her chair in against the desk and make sure that he had no opening in which to distract her, but, alas, things were not quite that way. Whether that ended up to her benefit or her detriment, however, was up for debate.

She tried not to grunt, holding her worry in her throat as he wriggled under her desk. Did he think that he'd dropped something down there? She tried to move to the side, to give him room, to let him work his way out as soon as possible, so that she wouldn't be distracted on her call anymore.

"Oh!"

"Melanie, are you alright?"

The conversation paused and she swore she felt every expectant eye turn to her in the Koom call, even if the head of sales, as always, was still, very obviously, on his mobile phone when he was meant to be one of the most important people on the call.

The feline blushed, shaking her head, though what she wanted to do was to nod. Yet what else was she supposed to do when her boyfriend's fingers had just brushed oh so tantalisingly over her panties, right up between her legs?

"Er... Yes, so sorry – there was a fly."

She smiled brightly, hot in the face and shooing Sam away under her desk. What was that cat thinking? She couldn't do something like that on a work call! Was he so bored that he had to come in there and bother her?

The feline, however, only looked up at her with a cheeky look in his eye that promised trouble, Mel with one eye on him, one eye on the screen. She couldn't pay attention to anything that was going on, however, not with him down there, not with her breath catching and hitching in her chest, his fingers trailing and dancing up her thigh.

It was tantalising, so very much so, enough to make her heart pound, a fixed smile on her face, chin propped up on one paw. Mel drove her knee into his chest, more sharply than she thought she needed to, but she didn't know what else she could do to get him to stop. In hindsight, perhaps saying "no" would have gotten him to stop, yet the feline was not thinking clearly, not as her chest warmed, the hitch in her chest tighter than before.

It was wrong...but the meeting was so boring. Maybe she had been more bored than she had realised, considering how all had ended up, his fingers pressing lightly against her folds, tracing down them while she did her best not to show any reaction or emotion on her face. Mel's whiskers quivered, wanting to mewl, though her partner was relentless, kissing her bare legs, the softness of the fur there tickling his lips. He knew how to get her going between than anyone and, perhaps, there was something in Sam that had told him that Melanie needed "it" more that day than ever.

He knew her. Likewise, she knew him. Even if she didn't always think that she wanted everything that Sam wanted, all the time.

Slowly, so slowly, she parted her legs for him, her willpower fading as his finger curled up inside her. Inwardly she cursed herself, her weakness, her fallibility in falling for Sam's tricks once again, though the feline between her legs appeared qu te like the cat who'd gotten in the cream. He murmured against her pussy, his purrs rolling softly into her body, her hips rising, rocking and thrusting against him. Under her, the computer chair squeaked, yet it did not get picked up by her microphone, thankfully, the headphones tucked down neatly on top of her head, covering her ears. In the required style for most anthros who needed to use them, they were tipped back, considering that her ears were not down on the sides of her head, but on the top.

It was a strange thing for her to think about, nodding and smiling at the screen and the webcam as she spread her legs for him, wondering why she was suddenly being so bold. It was not for her, not when her heart pounded so wildly, not when she wanted to be professional, but it was hard for her to say no as he tugged her panties aside. Maybe things could have been completely different if she had not worn a skirt that day, not allowing as easy access to her pussy, but that was well and truly out the window, her tail curling back and forth as his breath washed over her bare folds.

She was already slick and wet, marvelling at how her pussy was soaked, her lips surely glistening with her arousal. She imagined what he saw under there, the desk blocking out most light, yet her whiskers quivered obviously as he lapped up her pussy lips, holding her panties out of the way to the side with his paw.

"Mmmph…"

"Melanie, sorry, did you say something?"

What were the odds? She shook her head and gave a fake laugh, saying something about not making a sound, though she would never have thought that they would have asked her if she was alright or if she was trying to contribute. More often than not, others talked over her when they were on Koom calls, though not that day. That day, all eyes seemed to constantly dart back to her, Melanie more of a focus than anyone else on the call was.

That was solely her imagination at work, though Mel could only do so much, grunting and panting, whimpering softly as she rolled her hips up to Sam, pushing the microphone on the headset away from her mouth. She faked and pretended to be fiddling with her settings, frowning at her computer. It was a ploy and a half, but she could only hope that it gave her a little cover for her distraction, clawing and scraping at any idea possible that could give her a reason, after the call, for why she was so distracted during it.

She couldn't ask Sam to stop, not as pleasure zinged through her veins, her body aching for it. How long had it been since she'd last gotten off? She did not know, could not say, panting through her nose, clamping her mouth shut, but she couldn't seem to stop her nose from twitching. She was like a damn bunny with their twitchy-twitchy noses, rubbing her face, pretending to stifle a sneeze.

Yet the warm lap of a tongue over her pussy, despite the risk, was the best respite that she could ever have hoped to come out of a boring work call. His tongue slipped between her folds, dipping into her, tickling her clit, though the ecstasy that thrummed forth from that touch was more like the string of a guitar being plucked, trembling with delight. Her whole body ached for it, wanting to do more than the lightest of humps up against his muzzle, but she was trapped there, oddly luxuriously so. It was a kind of bondage all on its own, even if there was not a single rope or handcuff in sight.

But why was it so hot?

"And for the first quarter of the next year…"

Oh, were they still going on? She was only glad that they weren't asking her to talk, her nose tipping from side to side, striving to shrug and release a little of the tension in her body. It was all she could hope for, as hopeless as it was, his finger teasing up, slipping inside her, a second digit added soon after.

She tensed, suppressing the urge to cry out. God, that was good… So good… She had to get off and she had to get off soon, feeling as if her whiskers and fur were about to burst from her body, combusting in a flare of flame. She was too hot, squeezing her thighs around his head, the feline down there playing his tongue over her clit, lapping and teasing, even suckling on it firmly when he *knew* that she couldn't take pressure like that for very long.

Yet, in such a position, Mel had to. She could not lurch to the side and shove him away, putting on a face for the video call, her expression far from neutral but passable enough. He had well and truly trapped her there as her pleasure mounted, increasingly, every moment that passed pulling at her, tugging her desire onward.

She had to have it, couldn't hold on for much longer, her breath warm in her throat. Even Mel's lips parted as she breathed through her mouth, taking the chance and muting her microphone, even though she knew that they were not supposed to do that for meetings. She could only hope that no one there would notice or decide that it wasn't a big enough problem to call her out on, not even as her toes curled and flexed, rolling her hips up while still seated to allow her partner easier access.

"Yes..." She breathed, praying that she was indeed muted, fear pulling at her in the lure of mounting orgasm. "Yes... Oh... Sam..."

Whether or not she was muted – her orgasm was coming, a roar of pleasure swamping her, her pussy slick, so slick, wet and dripping down his fingers. She was not able to keep her expression completely plain, giving one cry as the meeting droned on, though it was with deep gratitude that she did indeed see that her microphone was, blessedly, muted, and no one heard her climaxing on her boyfriend's fingers and tongue.

He played her body wonderfully, teasing and drawing at her, fingers pounding her pussy, though it was only later that Mel noticed that he had added a third digit, sweetly stretching her out. She was tight at the best of times, yet that was just how her body was, squeezing around his fingers as if they were a thicker shaft, wanting that too. She could not deny that she was already a lot more relaxed even as the meeting wound down before her, her pussy rippling erratically, muscular contractions beyond her control. Yet who could have ever cared about losing control in a moment as sweet as that one?

Her climax left her warm through and tingling, melting down into the chair as she tapped her boyfriend on the head and, shakily, unmuted the microphone, murmuring goodbye to those on her team. They were wrapping up, after all, and the cat felt quite as if she could have used a good lie down after such a good orgasm. No one would know when she was working from home!

"Melanie, did you take down all the notes you needed? Melanie? Mel? Are you listening?"

Notes? Her brow furrowed, panting lightly, lifting a paw and half-shrugging at the camera. It was not as if she could do anything about the notes that she hadn't taken, not as her boyfriend purred up from between her legs, hoping that the microphone near her lips did not register the sound.

"All good, boss, sorry about that," she said, as breezily as she was able. "Sound just cut out there for a moment – sorry!"

Everyone nodded, saying their goodbyes to one another, some even splitting off into smaller, separate meeting rooms online for small talk and catching up: something that had become more important than ever for the remote team. Yet all Melanie could do was fumble and sign out of the call as quickly as possible, slumping back in her seat with the tightness of her underwear against her thigh, her boyfriend slipping his fingers into her pussy once more, tasting and teasing out a drop more of her wetness.

"You, Sam," she grumbled, though it was good-natured, "have a lot of explaining to do."

Sam blinked innocently at her. She rolled her eyes. Was there anything that that cat could deem innocent in the slightest? Probably not, though he did try and tugged at her heartstrings in ways that no other partner of hers ever had done.

He purred up at her, licking his lips as if there were still a few drops of her cream lingering there.

"Well…" He murmured. "You didn't seem to mind it all that much. Round two, sweetie?"

She leaned back in her chair, scooting her hips a little closer to the edge.

"God, yes…"

If there was one way to work from home, that was certainly the one that Mel wanted to keep on with!

Aquatic Pleasure

Coral's name, well, was rather stereotypical for a dolphin anthro, but she didn't mind it, not all that much. Like many of her kind that went about most of their lives on land, she had legs, though swimming "just like a dolphin" was of no trouble to her, her smooth, grey body cutting through the ocean like an arrow loosed from a quiver. She'd learned that expression when she'd taken up archery: something that no one had expected of her.

But she preferred being out in the water too, dipping and flowing through the open ocean, further from land than any land-dwelling mammals would often go. And she had found the perfect partner, for her, in a beluga named Kygo.

Kygo chattered softly, clicking as he sent echolocation out, though he could see well enough, considering that the anthro beluga whale's eyes had adapted to life as an anthro too, developing over thousands of years. At least, that was what they had learned in school. He was far more eager to spend time with Coral, out in a little secluded cove, as he flitted around her underwater, his swim trunks rippling and flowing with the lightness of the ocean all around him. Like the dolphin anthro, he had a blowhole positioned on the back of his head, though sometimes too he did take in air through his mouth. What he did not have, however, was nostrils, something that his friend, Sam, a wolf anthro, was forever teasing him about.

He streamed bubbles, guiding her in from the open water, smirking a little, though Coral gave him as good as she got, speeding past him with a flick of her long, powerful dolphin tail. To be fair, he did not quite have the speed on him that she did, even though he spent much more time out in the water than the dolphin, but the beluga would never feel bad about that. Not when she made his heart sing so.

And Coral was making other parts of Kygo's body sing too at that time, the slit at his crotch parting slowly, revealing the throbbing length of his pink shaft into his swim trunks. The bulge there rose, though she did not notice it, not until he nuzzled up against her, letting the full length of his body brush up against hers.

Coral grunted and looked back at him, a smirk on her dolphin beak. Oh, so that was how Kygo wanted to play it then? She flipped over, brushing her tail over his smaller beak, the mouth that was designed to catch larger prey than her beak would have been. She liked fish, but was better suited to grabbing faster, more agile prey than he was, though they didn't have to worry about things like that, not as anthros.

They could worry about other things. Like how the barrier between the sea and the sun glittered above them, no one else out there in the water than them, the sparkling, dancing layer separating them from prying eyes, from the outside world. She chirped, bubbles flitting from her blowhole, silvery, streaming towards the surface, and he came in closer, beak parted in a smile.

Ah. His eyes still crinkled in at the corners. It was funny how that never failed to make her heart leap and jump in the weirdest and most wonderful of ways. He had so many little quirks about him, but she had fallen for his kind nature, how Kygo so very often went out of his way for others. Sometimes, that needed to be tamed back a little, even when it came to her, but she would forever hope that she brought out the best in the beluga whale where she thought he really did bring out the best in her.

Even her cheekier side. Coral flipped and chattered, water swirling around her, a bed of coral beneath, though they were far enough above it to not have to worry about causing any damage. Aquatic anthros like them were some of the least likely to cause that manner of harm, after all, but she tugged her bikini bottoms, neatly covered up, aside, showing him a flash of her backside.

He was on her in the blink of an eye, making her giggle, neither dolphin nor beluga straining for air yet, though they would be in a few minutes. They couldn't hold their breath forever, after all, no matter how much they may have wanted to. He pressed up to her, holding her from behind, swimming together, finding the time and the rhythm of their tails pumping the water together, powering them through the water.

In the distance, the water was murky, not allowing them to see forever, though they dodged shoals of flickering, colourful fish. Unfortunately, their names eluded Coral as her boyfriend ground up against her, a decidedly hard length grinding into her backside as she chattered and chirped. They did not converse as readily in their old language, not anymore, but it was more than enough for her to show her readiness, pressing her tail back against him and reaching back to tug the waistline of his trunks down.

The beluga would have blushed if his skin could contain that hue, even though he was pale enough, cool water flowing over him, caressing him from head to toe to tail fin. He had other, hotter, things on his mind, however, like the round buttocks of his girlfriend, how she arched so beautifully back up against them even as they swam. They hadn't fucked in open water for a good while, but that morning seemed as good a time as any, twisting and turning together, dipping over a kelp garden just to let the long, satiny fronds caress their bodies.

Kygo helped Coral out by freeing his erection, though they already knew the intricacies and nuances of one another's bodies to fuck like that, most comfortably. Yet he would have hissed through his teeth (though it would have come out of his blowhole, most likely, in a rushing puff of air instead) if he had been able, grinding against her backside. He needed her and, evidently, she needed him too as his cock slid over her slick, smooth skin, their bodies begging for pleasure.

And who would Kygo be to not allow her that? He slipped inside her, finding her tightness and bearing deep, her legs coming apart a little, faltering, drifting, wavering in the water. Yet it was a good thing indeed that her tail was separate from her legs, sprouting from the base of her spine, thickly pumping through the water to keep them swimming together, though it was something more of a jolting, juddery swim than what he had been anticipating before. With his cock inside her, however, he could pump and thrust, filling her smoothly, sweetly, stroke after stroke.

He moaned, pressing against her, though the smooth round of her head could not squeeze back against him as he wanted. No... Not while they were swimming, thrusting, humping, every thrust of his cock spearing into her hot, tight pussy. It was not wet, per se, but she was slick inside with her own arousal, allowing him to pump deeper and deeper, using every inch of his cock that he was able to.

Coral groaned, relaxing against him, slowing the pumping push of her tail to a better pace, though he was better designed for swimming more slowly than her, even if they still came together well. Need tangled between them like kelp around their tails, skimming the top of the coral reef as fish danced around them.

That was all she wanted. Her mind drifted. That moment of being, simply being, connection with another human being. She blew out air through her blowhole in another stream of bubbles, his cock sliding deep into her, though she ached to feel his hips grinding all the way up against her. Maybe they would have to go out for dinner later that night and back to hers, just to take some even more private time together?

But that was a thought for later, not when her boyfriend was so very naughtily filling her out there in the water. There could have been anyone around, boats passing by – and yet no one would ever see them, not unless they swam directly by. So close to being uncovered and so free from being discovered… It was an intoxicating touch of lust and passion that Coral had never before gotten to enjoy.

And she would, time after time again, with Kygo, all with the beluga whale. Maybe even for the rest of her life, if she was exceptionally lucky with him, for he really was the light of her life.

She grunted, wanting him harder, wanting him deeper. And yet, that time, she couldn't tell him that that was what she wanted, her heart pounding, blood rushing around her body with ever-increasing fervency. The cord of tightness pulled more and more within her body, closing inside her, and she squeezed around him without even thinking about what she was doing, wanting more, every inch of his cock that she could possibly get inside her.

She needed it, even though she couldn't tell him, and was bolstered through it all by Kygo thrusting harder, filling her sweetly, her head spinning with pleasure. Slowly but surely, the need to breathe pressed in on her senses, coaxing her to pay just a little more attention to her lungs, yet that was not right for the moment, oh no. Not then, now when the spire of his cock crammed her full, the urge to breath snapping, pushing, prodding and pulling, right at the back of her mind.

Kygo didn't want to come up for air either, not until they were done, his arms tightly wrapped around her, though the beluga was not quite as careful of the dolphin's dorsal fin as he could have been. His lust was just so great, pressing in, thrusting, grinding, lost to passion as she bucked back against him, the two of them hardly even moving through the water at all.

If he had not been with Coral, the beluga would have ducked back to the surface quickly to take a breath, to refill his lungs...and yet it didn't seem to be an option in that moment, not anymore. Not as her pussy was squeezing and pulling, even if erratically, so delightfully around his cock that he just had to keep driving on, the pressure of the water moving around him in time with the force of his thrusts. There was resistance there, yes, but that was part of the beauty of swimming, how their bodies slipped through it smoothly, as much a part of it as any creature could ever have found it possible to be.

They were there and they were anthros, yet a kind of anthro that, perhaps, never truly needed to grow legs. But that was long gone as she spread her legs wider for him, taking Kygo deeper still, her pussy squeezing suddenly. For nothing at all would have ever stopped the dolphin from bucking and humping against him in orgasmic bliss, passion coursing through, throb after throb and pulse after pulse. She milked him for every drop of cum that his internally held testes could have possibly had to give, stroking down the length of his cock – and Kygo simply could not hold back.

He bucked against her, ejaculating crudely, pleasure swamping him even as the pressure on his lungs tightened and tightened. Though the dolphin was already swimming upwards, taking him back to the surface with her bikini bottoms clinging to the side of his cock, his trunks shoved down and partially off, even as he spent himself inside her. With Coral taking care of him like that, just the way he liked and needed her to, he could relax into the moment, truly revelling in each and every spurt of cum that left him.

There would be nothing for him to worry about, with spending his cream inside her without anything as a barrier. The dolphin had already taken care of that and Kygo smiled and pressed his beak to the back of her head in a silent kiss as his lungs burned and Coral took him all the way back up to the surface.

Aquatic pleasure had its upsides and downsides…but there would only ever be good sides left for Kygo, as long as he was with Coral.

Maybe he would have to dive for that pearl ring for her after all…

The Werewolf's Lover

It was easy to fall for her, how her bare skin felt against my teeth, poised so delicately, so carefully, at her throat. One snap of my jaws could have severed her neck, blood spurting, delicious. But I would never do that.

I loved Amelia too much.

Her bedroom was large with a four-poster bed and wall hangings draping elegantly, the castle expansive, though it was nowhere that a werewolf should ever have been present. It was for a queen, a royal, a princess – someone of high class and birth in the world. As a potion maker, I was no more than a commoner in comparison to her. Still, she said she loved me all the same and I was prey to her wiles, her tender touch, the stroke of my fingers over the back of my neck and down my shoulders.

I kissed her fiercely, passionately, a long tongue snaking into her mouth, claiming her as I felt she had claimed me every time. Yet that claiming came in two parts, giving equal parts of ourselves to one another.

She arched up under me with the touch of moonlight on her pale skin, her blonde hair falling in light curls around her shoulders. If I was the devil then Amelia, most certainly, was an angel, an angel laid out before the werewolf that I was like a feast to be devoured.

And I couldn't resist her.

"Oh... Samuel..." She breathed, eyes alight, kissing my nose, down my neck, into the thicker fur there. "That feels... Oh..."

I licked my lips, looming over her, my prick hard and ready... but where was the sense in breaking the moment so swiftly? We had come together in passion, on the full moon when I transformed, too many times over to count – and even more times when I was in a human form.

No... No. I would wait, I would tease, I would please. In her hands, I was nothing more than Amelia's sweet puppy, though I was chained to her willingly and moaned as I kissed and lapped my way down her chest and stomach, the hair of my muzzle tickling her gently. I wouldn't have wanted to be anywhere else and she treated me well, as an equal, going through town with me on dates, picnics, taking our leave on the veranda for a walk or two or three. Anything that normal couples, courting couples, did together we did too, as if I was not the werewolf that the entire town and beyond knew me to be.

It was a good thing that they did not put a price on the heads of werewolves anymore I was only shunned, made an outcast.

But my sweet, fair-skinned Amelia did not care and I wanted to show her, once again, how much I loved her, adored her, appreciated her for all she was, everything she had been and all she would become too. Her past, present and future were all that shaped her as she stepped forward, boldly, into the unknown of the next day. Sometimes I wished that I could be as bold as Amelia.

"Oh... Samuel..."

I loved when she used my full name, kissing her stomach, resting there for a moment. Maybe one day we would have a child, though I feared them being born a werewolf too. As many times over that Amelia told me that it was a blessing not a curse, in the glow of the moonlight, I didn't believe her. I didn't want to inflict my curse on anyone else, least of all a child that she birthed with our shared blood.

I nuzzled softly between her thighs my tail lifting and wagging, accepting that part of my wolfish body. I did not stand like a human, a bit more hunched over, my spine with a curve in it, digitigrade legs and pushed up onto my toes to walk. It was a good position in which to run and that was one part about being a werewolf that I did like, how natural it all felt being out in the wilds. My shaft pushed out against my sheath, bulging it lightly, though the tapered red length ached for her.

My tongue, however, was a far better treat as it snaked across her folds, lightly moistening, dampening, teasing. I had to ease her open, for it was my favourite way in which to start things, to slurp up into her softly, to seek out every sensitive spot she had in her with due delight and diligence. Her hands clung to my head, stroking over my fur, my ears, but I leaned into her even more readily, once again marvelling how small her body was compared to mine. It was a miracle that we even fit together at all.

Amelia's moans rose, pleading for me to go on, as if I was going to stop. That would not happen, not as I drank down her honey, the nectar on my tongue so sweet that I could not stop lapping up inside her. My tongue sensually dragged back over her clit with every stroke, curling around, sweeping and licking, though I wanted more, so much more, to feel her thighs close around my head in the delight of the moment, a throbbing, pulsing ache that could only be derived from the passion between us. Even my hand would never be anything at all in comparison to hers, her sweet mouth and the tightness of her sex wrapped around me.

It wasn't the same when I was on my own, seeking companionship for lust and love, rather than satisfying myself. Amelia grunted, appearing unladylike for a moment, but I loved her even more for that, for showing that side of her that was not a noble, that was vulnerable, that only came out like that with me.

"Oh... Yes... Ohhhh!"

She cried out and I bore in, forcing her over the edge, deeper and deeper, my tongue lashing inside her sex as if it was never again to be dragged back out. Amelia clung to me as if I was a lifeline in a storm that threatened to rip the roots of the age-old oaks in her castle grounds from the soil that they had dug into for centuries, squeezing around me, clinging to me. Her fingers dug in, but I didn't feel any pain, too caught up in pleasing her, the hypnotic grind and thrust of her hips up against me.

Her juices too... Oh, she was all the sweeter when orgasm took her and I hungrily lapped at her pussy like a wolf possessed, not even with the manner of refinedness that a werewolf could boast, if that could even be said at all. I let her ride out my muzzle through climax, my nose crushed passionately to her clit, though I'd take any pressure there, however firm it was, as long as it meant pleasing my lover.

When she sprawled out, panting and heaving, on the bed, I slipped up behind her, turning my sweetheart onto her side, her back to my chest. Her legs tucked up a little before her, offering herself to me, her folds exposed, the tip of my cock still aching as much for her as it had the very first time we mated. It was a soft position, one where I could not thrust too hard, but where I could stay as deep as possible, letting the rhythm and pulse of our bodies bring us to another sweet high.

Some expected werewolves to be rough. I could be like that if Amelia wanted it. But long, slow sex was my favourite and always would remain such.

I pressed my nose into her hair, inhaling deeply, the scent of rose and primrose tickling my nose, burying my muzzle there. It was where I longed to be, where I needed to be as she whispered my name and, slowly and gently, I sank into her. My length slipped inside her slick entrance, pushing on, the shuffling adjustment to my position hardly elegant, but it was good enough to get the job done.

Amelia moaned my name, pressing back against me, though she had put herself in a vulnerable position, where she was hardly able to get away easily. She could not grind back onto me, shivering as she delightfully took every last one of my long, slow thrusts, using every inch of my cock that I could while the unformed knot at the base tingled, that part of my shaft extra sensitive. If I was running my hand up and down my cock when I was alone, needing to relieve a quiet need, I would need to squeeze it to orgasm, mimicking a tying together with the knot.

With Amelia, however, that was not needed, not as I nipped and nibbled at the back of her neck, curling my spine to try to make space, my body more limber than one may have expected from a werewolf. But all I wanted to do was to be as close to her as possible, thrusting deep, hardly pulling my cock back at all as the knot began to swell, so slowly. There was no rush, not even as Amelia's breath quickened, her heartbeat racing so that sometimes I feared she was not enjoying the moment as much as I was, though I should have known from the first stroke of my cock that she loved everything I had for her.

Even my knot.

That had to be taken slowly, her breath hitching, one of my large hands covering her breasts, feeling like I dwarfed her with my body. I squeezed lightly, growling passionately, losing myself – but not so much that I forgot to care for her, to take it gently. My knot slipped inside while it was merely a soft round at the base, a bulge that could be taken, and she groaned, her chin tucked down, struggling even then to hold on through penetration. Once inside, I could allow it to swell more quickly, my body aching with a deeply seated sense of urgency, as if there was no time left, that I *had* to climax.

"Samuel..." She breathed, rocking her hips back as much as she was able, grabbing my hand, squeezing my fingers more fervently around her breast. "Take me!"

And, oh, how I did, kissing the back of her head, her golden hair clinging to my lips, all in the light of the moon, always watching, always waiting. My tail lifted proudly, my knot fully swollen, tying us together while it swelled inside her soft, accepting pussy, and I could not hold back as she moaned through a second climax. My cock must have pressed right up against her G-spot, sending her over the edge, the rippling, erratic contractions of her pussy around my length bringing me into bliss too with a barely constrained howl.

Against her, I could relax, throbbing, delivering every hot spurt of seed that I had into her pussy, how she tensed around me, as if, even then, Amelia wanted more from me, always more. I longed for that, for her to always want more, as if there would never be any true end to us coming together, that there would never be any final time, no last mating. If what we had together could go on until the end of days, I would be found a very happy werewolf indeed.

She settled softly against me, panting, her eyelids fluttering closed. The aftershocks of orgasm still rippled through her, around me, though tiredness pulled at us, making our limbs heavy, as if slumber would be the cure-all for our passion. The morning surely would find us as eager for one another as we always were and I sent a quick, quiet prayer up to those that may have been listening, thanking them for bringing such a beautiful woman into my life.

At Amelia's side, I would always remain. And her at mine, though I could not imagine what I had ever done to be so fortunate, so blessed. I curled around her, protective even in sleep, my muzzle twitching. In the morning, I would wake as a man again, my shaft soft, slipped from her, though our passion would be left as evidence on and in the sheets twisted around us.

The rest of my transformations, between the rise of every full moon, would be my own to control. I was only forced to be a wolf on the full moon.

Yet my darling let me be myself at any time.

My heart warmed, a low growl slipping from me as I joined her in sleep, tail wagging faintly, Amelia in my arms.

I would do anything for her.

Cream-Pie Slut

"Oooohhhh, yeah, give it to me, baby."

Crystal knew that what she was saying was cheesy, but that didn't matter, not as she arched back from the locker room wall, the musty smell of sweat and clinging musk heaving through her lungs with every snatched breath. The vixen whimpered seductively, the stallion behind her cramming deep inside, his hot length of meat pounding her, stretching out her pussy for all that would follow. She didn't know his name, only that he was one of those golden-coloured ones with a white mane and tail to die for, and that he was a damn good fuck. Slipping into the guys' locker room after her cardio session was just the perfect way to start the rest of her day.

Her fur was clean, for the moment, red and bright with energy and essence, though Crystal rolled her hips back devoutly into every slamming thrust. She didn't need to squeeze around a cock that large, the thick head pushing up so very deep inside her, so much so that she couldn't even take every inch of his cock. Maybe the vixen could have done so, with a little preparation, but the stallion was already doing a fine fucking job of grinding into her bare pussy, pre-cum slopping from him, thrust after thrust. The medial ring pulled at her folds with every stroke, popping in and out, though she yearned for more, the mess of it all spilling out of her, hot and creamy and so slick that it was not to be contained.

"Oh, fuck, you're... Unfff..."

The stallion groaned, his paws on her hips, dragging her back onto his cock as he climaxed, though the rippling pulse of her orgasm pulling through her was her delight, not his. But what else could the vixen luxuriate in other than knowing that she was going to be the best-known cream-pie slut in town by the end of the day? She milked his cock for all she was worth, his cock aching deep inside her, pulsing with every throb of lust he had for her.

And every drop was for her, her pussy taking it all, though some of his seed could not help, even then, but slop from her pussy. It drooled out, thick and wanton, marking the folds of her sex, dripping down her thighs. But Crystal had to try to keep it all inside her, right up where it belonged, her panties stretched between her thighs while her shorts were tugged down a little lower. Her crop top covered her breasts, revealing the bare expanse of her stomach and the white of her belly, her fur soft and clean, but not for long.

When his cock slipped from her, softening in time, she flicked her tail up and slid her panties in snugly against her soaked pussy, helping to keep his seed inside. It wasn't going to help in the long run, but if she clenched really hard, it might keep what she needed inside her for a little while longer.

"Nice going, stud," she chuckled, one eyebrow raised, her shorts tugged back into place. "Couldn't have picked a better cock and balls to start my day with."

Slumping against the metal lockers with a bang, half-naked and panting, the stallion blinked slowly at her.

"What?"

Crystal blew him a kiss.

"Don't worry about it, honey."

She didn't need to hang about, not when she could sashay out of the locker room with her bag over her shoulder into the leisure centre, her white-tipped tail flicking softly behind her. The weight of his cum inside her drooled and threatened to spill out, though she wanted more still inside before she let it all loose.

Where to next? The fox could go anywhere, anywhere at all, brushing her fingers down the arm of a cheetah who looked like he would be up for some fun, hanging out near a too fashionable shop with his branded hoodie tugged up over his ears. Maybe he could scent her pheromones on the air, how ready her body was to be bred and fucked, over and over again, or maybe she was just that influential. Crystal didn't care, as long as got every drop and every inch that she wanted from whatever partners were up for the challenge of pleasing her.

The cheetah kissed her passionately, lustfully, as if the moment was about to be stripped from him at a moment's notice, his tail ringed at the tip, lashing back and forth with raw lust. He didn't know her name and Crystal didn't have a clue who she was, though she needed him all the same, drawing his hardening cock from his jeans with a whimper of lust.

"Oh, yeah, honey," she cooed, her tail practically wagging with delight, even though she was a fox and not a dog. "Give it to me... You know what I want."

She made that quite clear as he hitched the flexible vixen's leg up over his shoulder, though Crystal would never quite have any recollection of how she had ended up with her shorts off, her panties dangling off one foot. Although she had her shoes on, all she needed was to press against him, more naked than the feline, though all that was forgotten as his cock drove into her.

Their heights matched up well for the position, though her hamstrings ached a little – it was something easy to put aside. She groaned, letting her head fall back, the cheetah's sharp teeth on her neck as he hissed, pounding her already sloppy pussy as hard as he could, knees bending and flexing for thrust after thrust.

"Mmmph, how are you...so wet?"

The cheetah didn't need an answer to that, not as his barbs dragged and pulled against her pussy every time he pulled back, though they had softened, not as they would have been for his species many, many generations ago. Furry bodies were better suited for one another than ever before and Crystal was glad of that as she took him like the pro that she was, panting and gasping, her tail trying to flag behind her, to show off her arse to anyone that cared to look. However, down the alleyway, there was no one to take note of her assets, her body, everything she had to offer as a willing slut on show, though she understood the need for discretion, solely to keep what was going on between adults only.

If she was going to fuck in public or on the edge of public, it was still important to remember herself, her values, all that she held dear. With as good as his cock felt inside her, making her mind drift away, pound after pound, her jaw clenched against a cry that threatened to spill from her lips in a shriek that would have most definitely garnered attention.

She had to hold it, had to cling onto him, panting, heaving, her breasts rolling with every gasp of air she dragged into her lungs, but she couldn't stop the force of her orgasm, the position making the fur of his crotch tickle her clit with every stroke. It was soft enough down there for her to lean into it, to want even more, whimpering as orgasm pulsed through her, stroke after stroke of his meat sending her to heights of delight unlike any other.

He was not long after her, seeing it as a quickie and not a marathon. But cats were very often quick off the draw, moaning into her neck as he bit and slammed deep, the slender tip of his cock even more sensitive than ever as he spilt his load inside her. His balls ached too fervently for him to hold back for a single moment more, tail swinging back and forth, the vixen smirking triumphantly as he added to the already sloppy, thick load of cum inside her.

And to think that he thought that she was merely just that turned on...for him? Oh, he was sweet. If she wasn't there to fuck and get the hell out of there, she would have hung about for a while longer. Maybe she would have even gotten his number.

But it was not what Crystal was there for, blowing him a kiss as she dragged her clothes somewhat back into place, though she bent over a little first to give him a good view of her arse and her sloppy, messy pussy before making good her exit. Cum drooled thickly from the flushed, swollen lips of her pussy, but the gape that had been left there was from the stallion and not the cheetah. The stretch, however, and the slickness left behind, had helped her take him and his barbs with ease. That was exactly why the vixen had chosen the stallion for her first cream-pie partner.

Maybe her last too... But not the same horse.

She slipped through the shopping centre in search of another, the sports shop catching her attention, though she would not hang about for a snicker at the balls or a crude joke or two that were, to be fair, right up her alley. Crystal was who she was, after all, a fox who was more likely than not to be found in some kind of athletic wear, perhaps running or playing volleyball, though she had begun dabbling in weightlifting too. It was amazing what a body could do when one put their mind to it.

That was why the vixen had to squeeze down on nothing, holding every last drop of their cum inside her that she possibly could, even though it was difficult, so very difficult. She swallowed a moan as she eased through the shop, glancing at shelves of shoes reaching to the ceiling, racks of clothes... Though they were not her prey, not her target. They couldn't please her like a guy could.

Well, no one could honestly say that she didn't have a type as she caught the eye of the cashier, a guy that she had had before and only remembered the name of because, well, he kind of had had a name tag every time they had done the deed. He was a thickly built moose with a full rack of antlers and, damn, he was hot, muscled but with a heavier, more powerful build, something of a muscle gut.

Crystal didn't care about abs though, not as she lured him into the changing rooms, the curtain sliding shut with a rattle after them. The moose, Troy, lifted her up against the wall, holding her, quite easily, in his arms, her panties strained to their limit as she tried to wrap her legs around him. But she was there at his mercy, panting, grunting, trying to be as quiet as she possibly could, his fat cock burying itself up inside the sloppy mess of her pussy, cum drooling from her thickly already.

But Troy was not under any illusion that she had not fucked anyone else that day, rumbling a low groan as his cock drove deep, the lewd squelch of his cock driving into her louder than even the changing room dividing wall rocking against her back. The thump of the vixen against it, hopefully, would not be taken as what it was, the two of them, once again, getting away with fucking rampantly, but Crystal wasn't sure she would have even cared if she had gotten caught. Maybe then she could just get on her knees down in the staff room or something and gotten railed by every member of the team, one hot cock slopping into her after the other.

He clenched his jaw, grunting deep in the back of his throat, dragging her back to reality, the stretch of his huge cock spreading her pussy wide. Damn, he was good, so good that the moose was one of the reasons that she kept coming back to fuck him, though Crystal would have been lying if she'd said that he was at all intelligent. He was not a smart cookie, not in the slightest, not in that way, but not everyone had to be a genius to be a damn good lay, after all.

He just felt too good pounding her, the milling about of other furs beyond the changing rooms barely catching her attention, though it was not as if Crystal would have cared if the damn curtain was ripped back and they were walked in on. She just wanted to be fucked and fucked again, each guy adding to the messy cream-pie of her pussy, how their cream drooled from her, leaving her a well-used slut who, still, after everything, was ready for more. To say that she was insatiable should surely have been an understatement.

Yeah, he had stamina, but the moose could not hold back as he ground into her, the urgency of the moment driving him into a frenzy. His cock pounded deep, stretching her out, slick and driving through the mess of her cunny. All she could do was weakly cling to his shoulders, swooning before his muscled might, Troy's antlers tilting to knock against the wall with a sharp rap with every thrust.

It wasn't going to stop them, not as he swallowed and forced down a bellow to the best of his ability, unloading inside her, ropes of thick, almost sticky cum flowing up inside her. It could not help but drool out around the fat length of his cock, thicker than the stallion's but not as long, though it fit her perfectly.

Damn, he was a good fuck, sending her blissfully over the edge too, though Crystal almost held back from that orgasm, knowing how weak it would make her legs. It did not soften the edge of her need in the slightest, still aching for more, so much more, even though she did not know how to take things easier, not when she was a fox on a mission.

Finishing inside her, his cock softened, the moose gently setting her down and helping her to re-dress herself all over again. The problem was him stopping to slide his fingers through the slick, sloppy mess of her pussy, teasing her with a finger, though it was nothing in comparison to his cock, curling up inside her against her G-spot. Against her better judgement, the fox stiffened and moaned.

"Oh, fuck…"

"Did you hear something?"

Troy chuckled and squeezed her backside as he left for a little damage control, though Crystal's need had already flared up thick and fast. She needed another guy and quickly too, any guy at all as long as he was down to dick her good and hard.

She didn't quite know how she managed to ease out of the changing rooms in one piece, her panties soaked, though she did her best, however that came through, to not allow her shorts to drip into the same state. That was not something quite under her control, however, not as she stalked out of the shopping area, heading for the nightclubs, even though it was only late afternoon.

Yes… A club or a bar… That would do, that would very much do, cum dribbling into her shorts, soaking her panties through, though they had hardly been made of thick material anyway. They had already clung to the shape of her pussy, highlighting her folds, her need, how it ached so fervently through her.

They knew her at one bar, a vixen's need legendary – even when it came to foxes always being down to fuck! The lights were half-on, purple and blue hues cast across the dance floor at the back, though she headed straight to the bar.

The bartender knew her, a lean but powerful wolf with an easy smile and a lift to his grey tail. He always seemed to be in a good mood, the pink of his tongue lolling out as he watched her approaching, setting aside the rag with which he was polishing the bar. He had something better there to capture his attention, most certainly so...

"Hey, guys – got Crystal up in here! Get your dicks out if you want to get them wet, hey?"

But she didn't care how they referred to her. It was all that she wanted and she even got free drinks and food out of it: what a total bonus for her.

The wolf took her into his arms, but there was no kiss to be shared between them as she was laid out on the bar, her head hanging over one side while her legs spread over the other. Her shorts could not hide the damp spot showing through for a single moment longer, though the wolf only chuckled and dragged them down, along with her panties, to reveal the hot mess of her cunt.

"Damn, guys... Looks like she's fucked half the fucking town before coming here! Girl, you know you only need to hit us up for a good time..."

The vixen smirked and winked, the wolf stepping one hind paw up onto a bar stool that was strategically placed for him to take a break behind the bar when it was slow enough. It also allowed him to get his hips up to the right level to drive into her pussy, his cock half-hard and out already, pushing the tapered tip against her soaked folds.

Her panties and shorts... Well, they weren't going to do Crystal any good anymore. Best she didn't think about those, wrapping her legs around him, dragging his hardening cock into her, though she only wished that she could get the knot too. She howled brokenly as he slammed into her, taking her as hard and as fast as she loved, her head tipped back and down so that someone else could slide into her maw. It was not quite what Crystal wanted, for a cream-pie could not slick down her throat, but it was something, her paws coming up to support herself against him.

An owl. Hm. Interesting. But he had a cock good enough to take her like all the rest, not even any balls held outside his body to slap off her nose, so it was not uncomfortable to take him as his firm shaft filled her mouth. Her tongue swirled around it, though Crystal was still more focused on the hot cock pounding her pussy, what load would come from those heavy balls, wanting more, always more.

And why shouldn't she get more? Even as more of the guys working there surrounded her, their cocks out, jacking off, making sure that they were ready for her, she knew that it was all for her. As much as she had to ask for it, to make sure her needs were known, she howled for it, moaning around the cock in her muzzle, upside down and looking down at a sea of legs. Her pussy tried to squeeze around the wolf's dick, but she could already feel his knot grinding up against the stretched folds of her pussy. He wouldn't be long, not long at all, but she wanted more, even if she couldn't have him knot her that time.

Crystal wouldn't get the luxury of seeing the heady cream-pie slop from her stretched, well-used cunt if he filled her like that, after all… Not with how long his knot took to deflate, which was something of a shame.

He slammed into her, holding back in the nick of time, his paw closed around his knot to squeeze it tightly, spending himself inside her. Crystal was barely aware of what was going on around her, throat bulging as she gulped around the owl's cock, more than happy to let the bartenders and other staff members use her as they pleased. For when the wolf left her pussy bare and free, cum drooling thickly from it, a cocktail of multiple males dripping from her, she was filled by a stag with a long, driving length of meat to match his full rack of antlers.

Oh, he was good, not a guy who had taken her before, even though he seemed to know and understand the "score" when it came to the fox. Treat her well, fuck her hard, be respectful – all that good stuff that made her fun what it was. Crystal moaned around the owl's dick, trying to hold onto his legs, but he thrust too hard and too erratically for her to find some sense of stability in the moment, her pussy used by yet another male.

She could not remember, afterwards, whether the owl shot his seed down her throat before or after the stag added to the mess of her pussy, but what she did recall was being lifted down from the bar, cum dripping from both ends of her. Set on the floor on her paws and knees, she rolled her hips back into the eager thrust of another fox, though he would not be able to knot her either, as delicious as it would be to be filled like that by one of her own kind.

More and more filled her, on all fours, then slipping down to missionary, her legs lewdly and crudely spread. A donkey, a bull, a badger, an antelope – oh, he was good fun, she'd have to come back and find him again – a bear and a lion too. Oh, the feral snarls, how they'd leaned over her, dominating her, luxuriating in her taking throughout everything, moaning and grunting as if they did not think they would ever get to take her pussy ever again. Yet they should have known that if they did a good job and filled the cream-pie slut to satisfaction, they would get all the pussy they wanted, time after time.

All they had to do was unload inside her...and what was so hard about that? One after the other, they relieved themselves, those that had filled Crystal already hanging around, lazily watching the show.

Eventually, however, the vixen lay flat on her back on the floor, cum drooling from her, dripping from her muzzle, even pooling around and under her tongue. Yet what she had really wanted was the sloppy mess of a cream-pie between her legs, spreading them wide with a low whine to show off the slickness of it, how much she had been stretched. It was why she had fucked everyone that she had, after all, why she had sought out more and more males to fill her, cum practically bubbling from her strained pussy.

Her folds gaped wide as if expecting another cock, the fur of her inner thighs and lower still matted and soaked with her juices, though the eye would forever be drawn back to her pussy, how cum drooled from it. The flex and weak push of her pussy gave the impression that there was something within her pussy forcing it out of her, but the fact of the matter was that there was only so much that her cunny could take, only so much that her body could do.

Who knew what would come of her time there, whether she would end up knocked up after such a kinky cream-pie, but it would never be exactly easy for Crystal to find out who the father was, if so. It was the risk that she loved, of having so much cum inside her that she felt more like a cum-whore than ever before, lusting for it so very much that she simply could not go without it, not in the end. And wasn't it her right too, very much so, to take what she knew she wanted, what she deserved, regardless of anything else coming to pass?

"Damn, I didn't think she could hold *that* much…"

"Is she still fucking horny?"

"Damn, Crystal, you sure you don't want to come back to my place later?"

She smiled, open-mouthed, enjoying the attention, all the eyes on her, not caring for the mess that seeped from her pussy. She was where she needed to be, after all, relaxing in the afterglow, letting them adore her body with their eyes, even though they zeroed in on her slick, drooling pussy, again and again.

They lusted for her. They couldn't help it. But that was why Crystal had come back to them, that time, making sure that those working at the bar got the best spoils of her stretched pussy, all in the use of her body.

For them and herself, she would always be a cream-pie slut.

But the vixen in question already couldn't wait for next time…

Public Bondage

Katrina squirmed, the gryphon delightfully trussed up in a gloryhole box on the high street — well, the high street of the red-light district, adults only allowed. She lay on a sort of padded bench with a black top, tail tied off to the collar around her neck, practically purring in her restraint, though her beak was gagged open with a chunky ring gag that would accommodate a range of sizes. Her brown fur and tawny feathers, spotted with black, could not be seen in the dark of the gloryhole box, though the gryphoness knew exactly where she was, wriggling in raw need.

Damn, she needed it, her beak trying to yawn more widely, though she was fixed in such a way, arms and legs bound to the bench, that she was positioned with her beak and sex at both holes of the gloryhole box. Even though she could hear other furries passing, late that night, she didn't know who was there, who was going to take her. And no one had yet made use of her dripping wet pussy yet…

"Unnfff…" Katrina groaned, desperately wriggling and squirming, doing everything that she could possibly think of to try to attract the attention of a passer-by. "Mmmph… Ohhhhh…"

She couldn't make many sounds, drooling openly through the gag, but she could try, her tail tugging at her collar, the long, leonine length helpless as her hands opened and closed reflexively. The heavy, leather cuffs left her exactly where she wanted to be, where she needed to be, though her breasts pressing into the padding of the bench, even then, made her want to hump and grind, to find that extra touch of stimulation wherever she could. But that was just one of many reasons that she had signed up to be locked into the gloryhole box for a night. Getting what she needed sexually was only part of it…

"What do we have here?"

A voice! Oh, she hoped they would use her, very much so, but the chuckle came before the touch of a hand, two fingers sliding into her sopping wet pussy.

"Mmmnnggghhh…"

She groaned, tonguing the gag, slipping down into sweet submission already. With her sight deprived of her and her body locked down, ignorant to all touch bar what she was given, every sense seemed heightened, the musk of a male flooding the nares on her beak as she shuddered in place. Oh, it was so easy to slip down, to not even listen to their degrading language above her, though she wanted it all, her pussy twitching and flexing softly around the fingers plundering her.

She didn't need to know whether it was a dragon or a gryphon or a canine or some other kind of anthro entirely who was taking their liberty with her. All she needed was to be there, to be used. And that was exactly what Katrina got as those fingers were replaced with the dripping head of a hard-on that made her swoon. Someone fumbled, bumping into her beak where the rounded top protruded through the hole, another cock teasing up against her, though they seemed a little more hesitant, shifting away and back again.

"Use the slut good…"

"Dude, you're really going to fuck her in public?"

"Yeah, well, you're fucking her beak, it's the same damn thing"

The next thing she knew was that she was filled from both ends, a delicious sense of fullness seeping through her as she gulped around the head of a hard, throbbing cock. It didn't even matter to Katrina who or what species anthro was taking her, only that she was there, that she could be used, that she couldn't do a damn thing about it even if she had consented to everything.

They fucked her swiftly, taking her in such a way that she hardly even knew where she was anymore. All that remained for her was sensation, the glorious squelch of a cock ploughing her needy pussy, her cunt already so wet around him. She'd been more than ready the moment she'd been locked into the gloryhole box, though it was not for her to know who was fucking her or vice versa. That was the beauty of it.

Katrina's head swum, helplessly trying to lap at and tongue the cock in her beak, though there was little she could do with the ring gag in the way. It kept the rougher edges of her beak out of the way of a fleshy length of meat, but it was still tricky to use her tongue with the gag, wriggling over and under, licking at what she could. She managed, just about, to get a drop of pre-cum on her tongue and let out a long, low, satisfied hum as she gulped it down, ignorant of the drool slipping from the corners of her beak.

"Unff... Such a fucking slut... Drooling for my dick."

"Her cunt is fucking red hot too. Damn..."

The male fucking her cunt sped up, his hips slapping her backside roughly, every grind bringing a fresh rise of sensation, pleasure mingling with a warming tease of pain, as if he was spanking her. The box trembled, though was thankfully bolted down so she could not be carted up and away, her pussy squeezing around his dick with as much force as she could put into it. He was a good size, enough to fill her, to stretch her out, but she wanted more, especially as the cock in her beak throbbed deliciously. It ached and strained in the heartbeat of a moment before the explosion, delicious ropes of thick seed flooding her beak.

She groaned and moaned and tried to savour every last little moment that she could, from the slick dollops landing on her tongue to the escaping sensation as it trickled from the corners of her beak. The other guy was not slow at all to make the same use of her pussy, unloading his full load into her with a low, deep groan.

"Ah, fuuuuck..."

Just there, just a sex toy, her pussy aching, begging, again, to be used. Only used. That was all Katrina needed, the cock gone from her beak even while the other pulsed within her, her fingers twitching, wanting to reach for him, to beg for more. It was her bondage that kept her in place, however, wonderfully helpless for every bit of fucking they wanted to put her through.

The messy cream-pie of her pussy drooled in the wake of his smooth length, voices fading, left alone for a moment. Yet no more than a moment as she was used again, fingers teasing into her pussy, an unknown anthro cursing under their breath.

"Ah... Damn, I prefer first dibs."

She crooned, begging for it, though her tail was not visible as she jerked it up against her bonds, striving to display her readiness. Her pussy ached and she keened out as shrilly as possible as she took him deep, a ridged cock plunging into her that time. It sawed back and forth, thicker around but not quite as long, tugging at her folds and raking divinely over her G-spot with every thrust.

It was just the right amount of pressure and she arched and bucked uselessly as she climaxed, lost there, lost to him, his driving cock, the male who was only interested in taking his pleasure from her and no more than that. He didn't need any more than that, not when her body was as primed and as ready to use as it was, heaving, grunting, panting heavily. She chanced that he had wings, hearing flapping through the dim haze of her orgasm, but Katrina could not be sure.

It didn't matter, not at all, not as he pounded her ruthlessly, taking her as if she was nothing to him – which she was. And that was the best thing of all as he spent himself inside her, a quick, short orgasm that came with the drive of urgent need behind it. Hot spurts of virile cum filled her, even though, in that instance, there was no chance of the gryphon falling pregnant. She still trembled at the thought of swelling with eggs, the children of another that she didn't even know the name of growing inside her.

It would be hot to think about though, what she needed as his cock pulled from her, voices bustling together, feet shifting, as if a crowd was gathering.

"Fuck, we haven't had one this tight in ages…"

"Must be a real slut."

"Like you care, as long as there's someone here to fuck."

"I'm going to take that beak while she can't clamp around me, damn…"

She quivered, waiting, though they were quick to move in on her, knowing why she was there. There was not a whore in the gloryhole box every night, but Katrina's heart sang to be that whore, that night. Her tail ached as a bigger, thicker cock again pressed to her pussy, sliding…up?

Smearing her juices from her pussy onto his dick, the unknown male used it to lubricate his cock for fucking her tight anal hole instead, not taking any sloppy seconds. The gryphoness keened, her whole body trembling, pulsing in a strange sort of orgasm, as if her entire body had undergone so much that it couldn't possibly be held back for a single moment more, heaving and grunting, a hot rod of flesh pounding her backside.

It drove deep, savagely, divinely. Or maybe that was her mind attributing even more to it, crying out through the gag, another dick that just barely fit the ring gag worming its way demandingly into her throat.

There, she was just a toy. There, she was just a slut. Fuck the rest of her life – that was exactly where Katrina wanted to spend the rest of her days! In orgasmic bliss, her pussy throbbing softly with pulses of blood, cum drooling from her, mixed with her juices. And the exquisite stretch of her tail hole pulsing around another cock, strained for the first time in a long while, trying to squeeze down but simply acting as a vessel, a lewd cum dumpster, for guys that wanted no more than to fuck her.

The gryphoness was barely aware of orgasm after orgasm sweeping through her, a cock swapped for another whenever any of the guys unloaded inside her, her pussy aching, craving it. Sometimes they took her tight tail hole, especially as it loosened for the bigger guys, though it felt as if a monster of a dragon took her one time, slamming in hard and fast, though his stamina was what made it for her. She'd cried out as two others had wedged in close together, perhaps bisexual boyfriends, to take her pussy and her arse at the same time, taking her with such timed passion that stars danced behind her lowered eyelids.

Heaven.

Ecstasy.

Was there any doubt in her mind that she would have stayed there forever if she could? To be no more than a gloryhole slut and everything that a gloryhole slut ever would need to be. That was what she craved more than anything else in the world, the passion of it, her head trying to roll back even as her bondage tightened and the collar dug deliciously into her throat at the front of her neck.

As a cock drew from her, leaving her empty and heaving for breath, if only for a moment, Katrina moaned. Cum streamed from her beak where the last guy had unloaded over her, giving her a half facial, though her head was obscured by the box, leaving her identity secret.

"What a whore..."

"I can't wait to fuck her... Move up!

All of them lusting for her, wanting her. Katrina whimpered, trying to grind back, to show them that her holes were still there to be used, that she was still the slut they needed her to be.

Use me.

Others milled around, lustful groans filling the air, closing in on her. Katrina shivered.

She would not be left empty for long. Not while the crowd hungered for her.

Another cock pushed into her dripping pussy, cum trickling from the soft gape of her tail hole, and the gryphoness could not help but moan. It was going to be a long, sleepless night, but the best of nights all the same.

She couldn't wait to see what the gloryhole box held for her in the dead of the night...

Storm Mating

Rain lashed down, striking the gryphon drake's feathers even as he spiralled through the storm, relishing in the grasp of the wind. As much as it strove to curse him down from the sky itself, he was not such a gryphon to be torn from the sky, ripped from it by the hand of God and laid down to rest, no. No, that would have been too soon, far too soon, for his time, his black feathers struck through with grey lines, though there was little detail that could be seen on his hybrid body in such a storm.

Ford snapped at the wilds, lashing out with his claws, exhilaration gleaming in his green eyes, though the gryphon had faced down such storms before. Yet he was not out there with his long, grey tail flickering behind, not much use in balancing the shift of his weight in such high winds anymore, for hunting or anything strictly necessary in his free life. He could do as he pleased, Ford pivoting on a hind leg, spinning with rain racing down his beak, as if even those droplets were trying to chase the storm and escape the solidity of his body. Yet there was nothing in the whole wide world and the mountain range that he loved so much that would make his heart pound as much as flying through the storm did.

The grey gryphon's hide trembled with power and muscle as he darted and practically leapt between lightning strikes, his head smooth like that of an eagle, the soft indents where his ears were keeping them nicely protected from the subsequent resounding booms of thunder. Amid the storm, it was all around him, skirting the underbelly of the clouds to remain where the storm languished the most, caressing his hide as if it yearned to tear it from him. Ford had never been a gryphon, after all, for a gentle touch, not when he could keen and shrill and dance, the sheath tucked up close between his hind legs plumping out with the rise of his cock.

Soon... But not quite yet. As much as the gryphon's desire churned in his aching nuts, dropping and making themselves more visible in the thick, yet soaked, fluff between his hind legs, he could not satisfy it quite yet. There was someone that he was waiting for, up in the eye of danger, threat all around. It was what made him feel the most alive, after all.

There was only one, out there in the wrath of the storm, who could match him, wing beat for wing beat. And that creature was not even a gryphon at all.

She was a dragon. Oh, how the rivalries of their species fell away as she shot into view, rain streaming from her large, leathery wings, beating droplets of water from them with every powerful downward stroke. Aventurine flew as if she was a part of the storm itself, the deep purple dragoness' scales struck through with splatters of deep blue, as if she had been splashed, though the trickles were forever fixed on her hide. Her long, balanced tail was tipped with a large spade, allowing her to direct her motion even more agilely through even the fiercest of storms, and her horns were long and sleek, following the line back of her skull down to her neck. On her body, as lean and powerful as she was, not an inch of her body was spared in anything other than the pursuit of agility and strength, of being every last bit the dragoness that she'd wanted to be since she could think, as a hatchling.

"Slowing down in your old age, Ford?"

She taunted him, though Ford wondered, sometimes, just how much of her taunting was good-natured. The nature of their relationship was not one that he could say he understood, as good as it felt, as if the electricity of the storm shocked through his veins with every flap of his wings and swing of his tail.

Yet he would not be shunned, nor would he be cast aside by his equal, chasing after Aventurine with single-minded intent, the rain lashing his beak. The cold of it did not chill through to his bones, not even at such a height, the mountains far below, even though he could not see them. If he fell from the sky, he would be splintered and dashed on the peaks below, becoming a part of the land once again before his time, though Ford had no intention at all of finding himself thrown to a sorry end.

Her tail whipped before him, the gryphon chasing the dragon with a gleam in his eye. He forced his way on, battling the wind that threatened to throw him off-course, though the strain of his wings held true and fast. More and more, his sheath thickened with his shaft, letting it slip out bit by bit. Of course, having that there in his excitement didn't help him make his tight turns or to be any more aerodynamic, yet it was the little yet important things like that which failed to matter at the peak of emotion. For there was no more intense scenario to play out before him, an active player in his own destiny, as Aventurine's tail flipped up high enough, only for a fraction of a moment, for him to see her slit.

It gleamed with rain and a drop of her moisture, yet the storm washed it away as soon as it was born. He moaned, licking the edge of his beak, wings pumping the air, shaping it to his will, even if the wind tore it away again a moment later. Oh, how he craved her… He remembered the taste of her sweetness, how it was like honey, but lighter, perhaps the dew from a flower only spreading its petals in spring? It was fleeting and it was tantalising, all in such a way that he ached more and more simply to claim her and it for his own.

Aventurine, however, was not to be claimed and neither was Ford the gryphon. He was free and so was she, divine beings in their own right, as much as his cock ached and throbbed, stinging with rain. He yearned for her, even if he could not feel her juices on his beak, not quite yet, the scent of her stolen by the wind. That was the only problem with the storm, even as it sent his feathers rippling, his guts twisting with desire: it took everything, whether sound or scent, from the air, leaving it all up to him and his imagination.

Though the gryphon pumped his wings, chasing her, closer and closer, following every whipping, darting line of her body back and forth. Her beautiful, rich scales called to him and he nuzzled up her tail even as she used it to balance. But they knew the lines of each other's bodies after so many times of coming together in the heat and the brutality of the storm, lusting for what they lusted for, even though neither gryphon nor dragon would have called the other their mate.

That wasn't the way of it for them. And it didn't have to be.

They had one another when they wanted them and that was enough. Not everything had to follow the standard twists and nuances of mating, after all, and they could walk to their path too – or fly to their own storm. If the storm and cheating death turned them on, well, that was all that it had to be for them, moaning and lusting, his beak pressing reverently up under her tail. He knew that she was groaning, the tiny reverberations travelling through her body not from the path of her flight but the tremors of her lust, his tongue lashing out over the slit of her vent.

She said something and yet Ford could not catch her words, the storm ruling, the storm overbearing. Ultimately, the storm would take everything that it needed from them, even as he clumsily flew too close to Aventurine, not allowing her any space in which to fly. Her wings faltered as he swiped up into her cunny, teasing apart her vent, though the pucker of her tail hole pressed up right under her tail did not escape attention too. It was not easy, after all, in such erratic flight to be overly accurate, not caring whether it was her vent or her tail hole that he pleased, each the same to him. The trembles of her body would come all the same, aching and shivering, a spark of lightning crossing before them, but not touching her scales.

Safe again. For a little while...

But they didn't need to be safe, not even as she slowed ahead of him. Her whimpers and moans were implied as he nuzzled into her, seeking the warming comfort of her body. Yet his cock ached so desperately that he hardly knew how long he could hold off for before he'd be mounting and trying to fuck her in mid-air. Sometimes they made it back to the mountains and the ground to fuck, but, well... That didn't usually happen.

They made it work, one way or another, Aventurine well-matched for him, though his tongue wriggling into her was all that she needed in the wrath of the storm, the thunder rolling through them. The deep reverberations coursed through as if the sky itself was howling, though they would come through it just as they always had, together, always together. Mates but not, the taste of Aventurine in his beak, always only her.

There was nothing else for him, not even as his cock throbbed, dripping viscously. Any drops of pre-cum that drooled forth were whipped away in a moment, slipping on as if they had never existed. Yet the taste of her pussy and how her tail hole puckered about his tongue made Ford drive on for more, pressing on against her, desperate for it, even as the first hints of exhaustion pulled at his wings.

He would not slow, no... Not yet. There was too much left for him, too much to lean into, grunting and groaning, letting Aventurine know in any way possible that he wanted her, body and soul. Even if they could only come together as partners in the eye of the storm, they would always have each other, the dragoness trying to bear back against him, though that was not quite possible in the heat of the moment. The storm was too powerful, battering their bodies back and forth, yet his beak ground ever more insistently against her sex, parting her vent, allowing her to glean more pleasure from him.

She arched her back, howling, struck as a silhouette, if only for a moment, against the poise of a lightning strike. Her orgasm rolled forth before Ford could even have expected it, juices squirting, painting his beak, rolling down her scales. Her hind leg kicked out, though Ford already knew that that would happen, dodging it neatly, the pounding of his heart sending pump after pump of blood around his body.

He needed it, needed her, and she needed him more than ever before as the storm raged, growing even stronger than it had been before. His need overpowered all that would come after, though they would not meet again outside the storm, not ever, not even the once. And that was just why he lashed out at the dragoness with his forepaw, lunging, turning her over, her eyes wide as he flipped her onto her back.

It was a move that they had played out time after time before and she knew it well, though it still took a well-timed snatch of her claws to capture his, flapping her wings, using them to power them along, even as she was upside-down. His cock ached and throbbed as he slackened his legs, allowing his belly to come closer to hers, even though Aventurine's pussy was still pulsing and rippling, her vent a little parted, in the afterglow of orgasm. One orgasm would not make the liaison, regardless of how it came about, but they only had so much time in the passion of the storm to come together.

Slowly but surely, he pressed down against her, the dragoness supporting them by balancing her wings across the erratic, buffeting gusts of wind, but Aventurine could not do it forever, not without him holding her up. Rain splattered down his wings, streaming in the worst deluge of the storm yet, the trembling roar of thunder echoing through his body. Through it all, his cock ached and throbbed, knowing that it was time.

They had to come together, the tip of his tapered cock, smooth with a light curve pointing up towards his belly in the shaft, pressing to her split. As if their bodies had been made for one another, they bred in the passion of the storm, one thrust filling her, the next bringing the dragoness to a storm-shattering orgasm. The gryphon drake hissed through a clenched beak, yet the storm ripped away his pleasure, slamming into her, though he could never be quite sure of how hard he bred her. All he knew was that he was left aching after their passionate liaisons. Seeing as he never saw Aventurine outside the storm and thunder and lightning, he could not say how well she fared afterwards.

But what Ford did know was that the ecstasy was more than worth it, a challenge at its best, their bodies meant to be together even if their souls were of dragon and gryphon. They were of different words, she and him, though they could always come together in the mighty roar of thunder, ducking and dodging lightning, cheating death and grievous bodily harm when there was no need to. How else, in a world that was otherwise so safe and sane for them, could they ever find out what truly made them feel alive?

His shaft plunged into her, shiny with rain and his own lubrication, though she was hot and wet inside. Her body was primed and ready for him to fuck and to breed and he did so fervently, for it might well have been the last time that they would ever come together. Neither of them knew, after all, where their lives would take them, from opposing clans, her body trying to arch desperately up to his even as she braced and strained to hold her wings out. They could not complete the mating dance of the storm, as the wind hurled them deviously from side to side, without her supporting them from the bottom, on her back. Without her, Ford would have been doomed.

Aventurine keened, his cock pounding her into another orgasm, grinding up against that part of her passage where he had sussed, before, that all the sensitive nerve-endings were located. It was like that for him too, the most sensitive part of his cock being the tip, so that he did not even need the thrusting motions bar for the pleasure of it, the raw savageness of breeding coursing through him.

Thrust after thrust slopped into her, pre-cum liberally coating her pussy, mixing with the pleasure of her arousal. He wondered if Aventurine lapped the cocktail of lust out of herself afterwards when she cleaned up, though he knew that she would not return to their storm dancing until she had grown fat with a hybrid clutch and laid them, once again.

He never saw her pregnant. She made sure of it. Yet that only made the gryphon drake lust for her more, the storm raging around them, her body gripping him oh so very perfectly as he buried his shaft inside her.

He keened out shrilly, rising back from her, wings flared, a silhouette against a cutting fork of lightning, yet it was too late for anything else as they dropped too sharply, losing altitude, wings flapping, feathers flying, his orgasm in full swing. It had not been something to hold back as he spent every drop of lust that he had felt his body had in it to give, internally held testis doing their best work as hot rope after rope of cum powered into her body. Mating in flight rendered their climaxes powerful and short, sending as much forth as strongly as possible, in the hope that it would reach the eggs of the female inside her womb.

He could only hope. And, so, Ford would hope, until Aventurine decided that she had need of his services in the storm once more.

Again and again, he thrust and thrust while they dropped, faster than the rain, wind howling, danger snarling. They had to come out of their freefall sooner or later as his cock softened, passion no longer needed, her eyes wide and wild, screaming at him to let go.

Yet he did not want to, not when it meant that he would not see the dragoness again for months on end, even if it was the only option available to him. There was no other answer, not as her sex squeezed around him, giving Ford one last throb of pleasure as he reluctantly slipped free and wrenched her to the side with just the one claw. That was a quick little movement, much needed too, that helped her flip back the right way up, though beating her wings and reclaimed her balance and height, safety as secure as she could make it in the storm.

The dragoness scowled at him, though Ford chanced that there was a glimmer of respect in her eyes that had not been there before. He had not clasped her that tightly prior, not in a way that said that he did not want to let go. However, he understood the nature of their relationship, why it was that things had to be that way. They were from different worlds, different species, but that didn't mean that they could not enjoy passion with them, his cock hanging out, slowly pulling into his sheath, though he was loathe to forget the gleam of her juices lingering there. It was a sensation that he never wanted to forget.

Shaking her head at him, Aventurine licked her lips, her lower abdomen surely heavy with his seed, drooling from her vent, the rain easing off. Yet their time there was done, come to a close, the storm howling without the same fervour.

It was time to move on.

"Until next time, gryphon."

He bowed, beak closed respectfully, hovering, the wind forcing him to exert more energy than usual to maintain his position.

"A pleasure as always, Aventurine."

He watched her tail disappearing into the storm, his cock barely retracting into his sheath, yet the gryphon yearned to see her again.

One day, when she wanted him again. It would all come. But Aventurine was a dragoness and a wild spirit who was not to be tamed…

Not even by him.

Light Bondage

"Ooof, Randall..."

Mina moaned softly, the moose shuddering on the bed, though she had never thought that the bed would be used for activities like that. Not with her arms stretched back behind her, the slotted, metal bars of the bed helping to lock her paws away, tucked into cuffs that she could not get free from. They were not the fluffy, soft ones either that could be found in the sex toy shops and around hen parties either – oh no. They were the proper, metal ones that clicked closed with such a decisive snap that the moose had practically creamed herself right there and then.

It was funny how such little things, like that, could make one feel so turned on, her skin prickling with heat, her fuller figure smooth with the curves of her body, from her wide hips all the way up to her large chest. Of course, her husband had already gotten her bra and panties off, which meant that they had had the desired effect on him, though Mina was glad too that she didn't have to replace them. Last time, he had ripped the fancy set that she'd managed to grab right off her. Granted, they hadn't covered very much of her body at all, but she had rather liked how they cupped her arse, slipping between her rear cheeks as if they were trying, even then, to grab her more deeply.

Some things were just hot to wear, especially for her, more comfortable than ever in her thirty-five-year-old body. Her husband, a brown bear, was not quite as ripped as he had been, but, well, that was all part of getting old. He had a bit more softness to his stomach than he had had before, yet there was still a strong round of muscle in his shoulders and upper arms especially, as well as down in his thighs. He took care to go to the gym frequently, even if his workouts, over the years, had become more of a mix between explosive sports, like squash, and his old, typical weightlifting. Something about the cardio being helpful...

And it did make him look good, for her, for anyone that laid eyes on the rugged bear, who stood a head taller than her: impressive considering her height as a moose. Even though Mina did not have antlers, she so very often felt her height acutely, as if she was smaller, as if she was weaker. As if she really could lean into the lust and the embrace of a big, strong bear taking his pleasure with her in the bedroom.

Testing her bonds, Mina played with a smirk across her lips as the cuffs held fast around her wrists. He had her where he wanted her, but the bondage, yes... She could stop it at any time, of course, if she only used her safe word, but the moose didn't want to, not as he pushed between her legs, his hard, aching length leading the way.

"Aren't you a beauty?" Randall rumbled, the bear lifting her legs, his brown-furred paws closing around her ankles and pushing them up, making her bend her legs. "And all hot and ready for me..."

Mina grunted and tried to arch up, to get him into her, but her husband was smarter than that. The bear hung back, just out of reach, his muzzle tilted to the side as he licked his lips.

"If you want me," Randall grunted, "you'll have to hold back. Can you be a good girl for me, Mina? Can you stay nice and still for me? Take every inch of my dick..."

He growled as she whined and grumbled and shook her head back and forth, though the moose didn't know what else she was to say to him. She wanted him, yes, but how the hell was she to stay perfectly still when his hard rod was there, waiting for her? Much less shoved inside her! Yet she gulped and swallowed, leaning into his game as he bent her legs up towards her chest, spreading them a little more.

Unfortunately, Mina was not quite as flexible as she had been in her younger years and could not bend her knees all the way back to her chest and bare breasts. She had done that before and, honestly, could have done so if she had spent the time on her flexibility, but, really, was there any point in that? Not when there were so many other things that the bear and the moose could do together, her cloven hooves beautifully kicked up in the air as he teased the head of his cock back and forth through the damp slick of her pussy.

Mina whimpered, turning her head to the side, no longer even able to look at Randall as the moose blew out noisily through her nostrils, puckering and flaring to contain her breath. Her bear knew what he was doing to her, oh yes, so thick and strong and dominating, pulling on a deeply seated need in the core of her being. She didn't think that anyone would be able to do that, other than him, though the bear's smirk was held back, dancing in his eyes.

"Mmmmph…"

She groaned, long and low, letting him support her legs, teasing her pussy. Only when the head of his cock brushed her clit did her hips jolt – but she didn't have any control over that, come on! That had been accidental, unintentional, she had not been able to hold it back, but he seemed to think that she could, that she could show him even more threads and nuances of sweet submission in bondage.

Mina quivered, settling back down to the bed as her arousal swelled, the need that she had not been paying due attention too rising with biting fervour inside her. She moaned, closing her lips to try to seal back her arousal, for the flow and pulse of it within her was more than the moose honestly thought she could handle.

That was, in the end, why she liked being bound. She could feel more, but, ultimately, she was not in control. She didn't have to be in control, not at all, not when she trusted Randall like that. And he would be able to tease her, please her, even as the bear grinned and slid just the tip of his cock into her wet heat.

"Unff..."

"You're doing so well, Mina," he praised her softly, yet the strong, velvety, honey-rich tones of his voice washed through her, making her tremble. "Stay still for me, my sweet little moose..."

Mina wasn't little at all, not by a long shot, but he made her feel small, deliciously so, even as he pressed into her. She huffed and puffed, desperate for climax, her large nostrils flaring larger still as she sucked in a deep, needed breath. Her chest heaved with the effort it took to stay in place for him and she wrenched discreetly on her bonds, hoping against hope that her husband would not notice.

If he did, maybe he would not fuck her like she wanted him to. If he did, maybe he would deviously tease and taunt her even more. All within their limits and rules, of course...

Mina didn't know what she wanted more, panting and moaning, a low, rumbling groan rising up from the back of her throat as if it simply was not to be contained. Oh, how she needed more, so much more, though she was forced to endure in her bondage, his cock sliding deeper and deeper, pressing all the way up inside her.

But not as quickly as she wanted it to. His paws braced on the bed, but he maintained incredible control of his body, though his arms trembled lightly from the strain of holding himself up such a fixed position.

Randall managed it, however, as the moose under him grunted her appreciation, the light aroma of sweat colouring the scent of her perfume in the air. Earlier that day, when she had spritzed it on her neck and the points of her pulse in her wrist, Mina had not thought that Randall, quite honestly, had something quite that kinky planned for her, but she didn't mind it.

She loved the bear's surprises. Especially when he rocked his hips in just the way she liked, adjusting the angle of his hips so that his cock pressed up even more firmly against the front wall of her pussy. She moaned, trying to stay in place, though the tiniest shift her own hips was still caught by the bear that she had loved and married – and still loved oh so very dearly.

"Ah-ah," he said, stilling finally with two-thirds of his cock inside her. "Don't move. I'll have to wait for that one, my darling..."

She shivered.

"Oh, please..." Mina whined. "Please fuck me... I can't stand it...like this! I feel you I want more of you!"

His dark eyes danced as he leaned further over her, his muzzle close to hers. Grunting, Mina tried to avoid looking him in the eyes but Randall forbade it, claiming her gaze with his own.

"You'll get it," he said lowly, his voice dropping another octave that made yet another needy little grunt break her lips. "When you are a good girl for me. Are you a good girl for me, Mina?"

She moaned. Damn it... He knew all of her weak spots. It may have just been roleplay between them, of course, something special for the bedroom, but she could not and would not have ever denied how hot under the collar he got her when he took charge. Frankly, Mina wasn't even so sure that the times when she took control too were something she was into. But that was something to talk to her husband about when she was not tied up.

Or maybe...

"Yes, master," she said, well and truly relinquishing every last scrap of control that she had to him. "Yes... Yes, I am your good girl, mmm... A good girl for... master."

It was not a term that she had used for him all that much before, but it seemed right in that moment, sending electric tingles of pleasure through her body. Even her tits trembled faintly with every breath, sensing the proximity of her husband to them even as he took full advantage of her form in the bondage, arms locked up behind her head. She moaned as Randall's eyes gleamed, though her words, blessedly, still had the desired effect on him, the bear moving again with long, slow pumps of his cock.

But it finally got the full length of his raging hard-on, throbbing and pulsing inside her, up into her pussy in the way that she wanted it to. She wanted him to thrust harder and faster, making her body ache with the force of his strokes, yet she knew too that Randall was drawing on another ache inside her, the ache of desire. The bear just wanted to rile her up into a frenzy, whimpering and moaning, bellowing with lust, though she would not break.

Well, not in the way that the bear had expected her to, that was. For all Mina thought about was keeping her hips down and in place, not grinding her hooves down into the bed to thrust up against him, to demand with the rock of her body that he fuck her properly. She didn't fold to the whims of him, even as the bear's strokes grew stronger, managing to prop himself up over her on one elbow just so that he could get his paw back down between their bodies, toying with her clit.

"Mmmmph," Mina moaned, fighting against every urge she had to twist her hips, to grind up into that sudden burst of electric pleasure. "Yes... Randall... Master... I need to cum so badly, please... Please, get me off, please... Cum in me!"

He smirked, though his chest rubbed against her breasts, so close was their proximity. Mina moaned as the fur of his chest and his strong pecs brushed her nipples. She didn't need all that heavy of a touch to feel good, just something, even if she would very much have liked to be pounded down into the bed as roughly as ever with his dick right then at that very moment. Yet her bonds held fast and she softened into sweet submission to her husband, letting him take her and use her body as he pleased.

Maybe that was the release that she had been looking for all along, taking every spark of delight she could get, from the brush of his fur against her nipples to the stronger pressure of his lower abdomen against hers as he thrust deeply. Mina fought and fought to stay in place, yet his pace picked up, cock filling her beautifully. There was a lot to say for a cock that thrust into her with just the right amount of friction, though the moose already felt that she had been soaked with need for him before anything had even gotten started.

"Mmmph, yes... Please..."

"There now, my little moose," he crooned, though even the bear was a little breathless as he plunged into her pussy, nuzzling under her chin and down to her neck. "That's what we're looking for, my good girl... You can cum when I say you can."

He didn't stop caressing her clit, however, keeping the pressure light enough so that she didn't orgasm too quickly and yet taunting her with the pleasure of it, what could come if only be buckled down and got to pleasing her as she so very badly needed

Mina puffed, snorting heavily, though her nostrils only vibrated from the blow out, the action not truly giving her any kind of release that would soften the tension in her body.

"Agh... No, I can't..."

"You can, darling, and you will. For me."

She nodded weakly, stomach twisting – in a good way. It felt like his words reached right down into her and curled warmly around the core of her being, what it was that made Mina who she was. Of course, that could not actually happen, but they did strike a chord within her that no one else ever had been able to, whimpering, lusting, her hips rolling faintly with his thrusts. It was soft and light enough, at that time, for the bear not to notice, even as he took his own pleasure, grunting and groaning with every strong, powerful thrust he took into her tight heat.

She couldn't help her breath catching and hitching, closer and closer to orgasm. She wanted to be free and yet relished in the restriction at the same time, though she did not quite understand why both could exist simultaneously. It was just delicious to tug and pull at the restraints, to be put in her place while knowing that she was completely safe with her husband.

But, no... No. Mina could not climax, not without permission, not even as the big bear thrust into her hard enough to cram every inch of his cock into her crudely, stretching her entrance and lightly tapping his balls against her with every thrust. Her legs weakened, wobbly where they should have been strong, but there was nothing she could do, not even feeling as if she was strong enough to grip him with her legs and beg her husband to take her crudely, to force her body over that edge into true ecstasy.

"Oh... Ohhh... Randall... I..."

"A little more... unff... a little more..."

He growled above her, showing his teeth in a brief flash of stronger dominance, and Mina swooned under him. The bear's hot breath pulled over her throat and clawed at her neck, as if he was actually sinking her teeth into her, and she allowed herself to languish in the fantasy, to let it wash over and push through her as if she was seeking out something even more tantalising.

And then he finally tipped over the edge himself, almost as if her husband had forgotten about her, groaning deeply as he kept his cock as far up inside her pussy as he could, powering into her with short, savage thrusts. His hips knocked soundly into her body with every jab of her hips back to him, bumping his fingers out of the way of her clit, and Mina would have cried out in loss, if not for the roll of trembling pleasure aching through her and the sensation of his cum flowing up within her pussy. It was more the trickles that oozed back out around the join of their bodies, around her folds and dripping lower, that she could feel, but the warmth of his load, of taking a prize from his balls, was something that the moose had always loved and longed for.

Through his growls and sharp grunts came three little words, however...

"Cum for me!"

She caught his words, just about, through the tenor of his need, and did just as her husband and dominant of the moment asked her to: she climaxed. It was as if her body had just been waiting for that cue all along, exploding into dazzling climax as her hips rocked up, bucking and jerking, need flowing through thick and fast. She cried out, panting for it, whimpering for it, needing it more than anything else.

The moose relished in climax, ecstasy throbbing through her, pussy clenching around his cock – but there was no rhythm to it at all, only raw need. And that was exactly the point that Mina had always wanted to be pushed to, where she couldn't even try to squeeze around him, completely at the whims of her husband and her own body, arms straining and burning from the bondage.

She moaned, riding it out for as long as she could, each wave of ecstasy coming with a different strength, always leaving her guessing as to how powerful the next would be and how long the next one would last for. But that did not matter, for it was not truly up to the moose to guess, her ears twitching back and forth as she swam in deep, lustful submission, her whole body warm and slack and loose from such a stringent high of bliss.

But it was okay. For her husband was there, his hard cock still throbbing lightly within her pussy, his strong paws smoothing over her fur, reminding her that he was there, that he was in control, that she was okay.

It may only have been light bondage but one thing was clear between the bear and the moose – and that there was far, far more for them to explore in the realm of domination and submission than they had realised.

Together, they would go as far as they desired.

Going for a Ride

The Lioness & the Stallion

Eda groaned, the lioness' head falling back as she ground up against her partner's cock. Truthfully, she had not met the stallion before that night, but the con was going strong and all of her friends had dragged her down to the bar and dance floor, all to get going and have some fun with those that were into their scene. Who knew that comic conventions and the like had such a thriving social scene? Though it did make sense too, actually, considering that that was one of the main places where everyone could get together with others that were on the same wavelength as them.

So, really, it was no wonder that sex and parties were a big part of such events, even though many would not have expected that. And people sure were ready to get kinky too...

"Unff... Yes... Arne..."

Eda grunted softly, but the black and white stallion under her blinked up at her as if he was the luckiest guy in the world. Which, to be fair, he was, as she purred and leaned forward, running her fingers and the very tips of her claws over his chest, pricking tenderly over his sensitive skin through the thin coat of hair that covered his body. Arne trembled, licking his lips, his muzzle a lighter shade of pink where his markings splashed to white around his face, a long, beautiful mane spilling down the arch of his neck.

Straddling him, the lioness was right where she needed to be, though she was thinking twice right then and there as she rocked her fleshy buttocks back against him. Sure, she was on the curvier side with a thick, full body, but that didn't change the size that she was inside and she had to say that he was a rather...impressive size.

The lioness blushed heavily, a little of the heat showing through the tawny fur of her face, even in the dim light of the bedroom. The bedside table lamp was lit, but it was one of those that had different settings – and it was stuck on the dimmest of them. It ended up casting long shadows across the hotel room bedroom as Eda groaned and pressed back against him, the stallion's paw coming down the front of her body to her pussy.

"Unff... Oh, yes... Mmm..."

"Tell me what you like..."

Oh, his voice was so soft and she could get used to that, how he was so very attentive to her needs and desires, how he was always looking at her, his eyes dark pools of liquid brown that she could see herself tumbling into forever. The aching pressure of his hard-on bid her attention, but his hoof-like fingertips – just harder with chunkier nails – on her clit, dancing and playing back and forth, were oh so very enticing too. Something like that was hard for Eda to get away from.

Still, she ached for something more, something deeper, the drip and drool of his shockingly over productive cock against her buttocks and lower back not something that the lion could so easily ignore, oh no. It was not for that, not as she bit her lip and lifted her hips, more than a little tipsy, but, well...that was all well and good when it came to that kind of fun. If she was fortunate, it would help her relax just a little bit more while she took him inside her, every throbbing inch and that fat, swollen flare too.

If he's that swollen now, she thought, biting her lower lip less than delicately as she knelt up as high as she could, pressing the flat head of his cock to her pussy. *Then...how big is the flare going to get when he actually cums?*

"Take it easy," he panted, nostrils flaring as his paws dropped to her hips as if Arne was trying to steady her. "Mmm... God, you're so pretty... You don't have to take me all in one go, or at all...if it's too much."

Eda snorted at that, the lioness rolling her eyes while she tested him against the plush folds of her pussy, feeling them give slightly at her entrance.

"You're not too big for me," she said, perhaps overconfident. "No one wouldn't fit inside me, you should...unff..." She eased down, popping the head inside her, nerve endings on fire. "Not...too...*big*!"

That last word ended on a yowl as she sank, determined to take him, though she moved too quickly as her legs ached and gave out, driving her pussy down onto his powerfully hard cock. Pleasure exploded through her and Eda was too far gone even in that moment to realise that it was all partly because he'd brushed her clit again, pressing down, stimulating her, not even relying on his giant horse dick to pleasure her. If she had been more in her right mind in that moment, she would have been impressed by that – a guy that didn't think his dick was the be-all and end-all of all orgasms.

Yet the flowing rise and pulse of orgasm pounding her, like the beat of the music that was surely still going in the dance halls ground through her, forced her to remain in the moment, to only think of pleasure, no more than that. For the lioness, there was nothing else, absolutely nothing else, that she could take for her own, electric thrills racing through her veins as if each and every one was trying to get to a different part of her body before any of the others.

"I got you, Eda, it's okay, I got you... Unfff... Oh, wowww..."

Yet Arne was not as in control as the stallion clearly thought he was, grunting and lipping the air, opening and closing his mouth even though it was not typical for equines to breathe through their mouths. His nostrils flared, sucking in breath, needing coursing through, though even Eda was in tune with the pulse and throb of his hard-on within her pussy. Despite his size and the rising bulge showing through her lower abdomen, she ground down even further, the medial ring popping inside her, though that was perhaps only since she was already so wet that she was just about able to take it.

Dry or unprepared, oh no... No, that would never have worked. Not for a dick like that, a dick that felt as if it was splitting her open from the inside out, straining her body, making her ache and pulse around him, muscles so very weakly twitching even though she was not trying to clench or even squeeze around his cock.

Eda could not have done so, even if she had wanted to. Never before had she had a cock that big and luscious stretching her out, her pussy so tight around him that it was a wonder that it had even fit at all. It should not have fit and, frankly, if she had not been as tipsy as she was, Eda would have spent more time working herself up a little more beforehand, though she had never, quite honestly, been a lioness who backed down from a challenge.

Coming down from her mind-blowing high, she sat up a little from where she had tipped forward across his chest, his paw on her pussy drawing a whine from her throat. Arne wasn't directly touching her clit, but had somehow found a way to stimulate around it in just a way that had her quivering without pushing past that initial barrier of oversensitivity.

Clever stallion...

She'd have to get his number after that, though, to be fair, they had spent a good time laughing and chatting at the bar over their favourite anime, so perhaps it was just all turning out to be even more of a match made in heaven than she had expected. Funny how things like that worked out, sometimes at the most unexpected of times...

Yet the moment was for her to take and her alone, chest rising and falling passionately, grunting as she ground down onto his cock. The bulge was immense, greater than she had ever seen before pressing out through her lower abdomen, even as she tenderly traced the outline with the tip of her finger. The lioness shuddered bodily, letting out a low, throaty growl.

"Oh, fuck..."

Arne was not much better, his legs bent as he gently rocked up into her, though her weight and position did limit him a little in what he was able to do, her pussy flexing around him. That muscular control, however, was well and truly out of Eda's control even if she might have wanted to greedily claim it, leaning wantonly into the embrace of Arne's paw and his cock burrowing up so very sweetly inside her.

"Are you sure...nngghh..." He groaned. "That...it's not too much?"

She purred, though it was hard to keep her voice level, rocking her hips on him as stars leapt and danced before her eyes, pleasure sparking right up to a brand new high.

"Only if you can take me too...ah...honey..."

She was blustering, acting more confident than she really was, but, well, if his cock was already over halfway inside her there was clearly nothing bad that was going to happen. That left Eda easily free to enjoy the ride, the slow, long grind and rock of her hips easing more and more of his cock into her, straining and stretching her open wonderfully, aching around his hot spire of flesh.

The stallion came along with her, matching her rolling thrusts as she pushed down onto his cock a little more each time, her pussy squelching around him, though the fit of his cock stuffed into her tight snatch was too great for anything to leak out. Every drop that Arne had to give, ultimately, was going to be forced up inside her – and with all their teasing and flirting so far, it did not seem like that was going to be very long at all, oh no…

Eda rolled with it, revelling in the sensation of being stuffed full, even if she had never before taken herself to be a size queen. That was something different, something very different, the ache and throb of a cock so much bigger than she could ever have anticipated pulsating inside her, as if she and Arne were connected in more ways than, originally, she could have anticipated.

But that was just for the moment as his aching shaft pressed up even more deeply inside her, the medial ring, somehow, pressing right over her G-spot. It was just a series of moments coming together too perfectly to be believed, yet everything was exactly as it was meant to be as her panting picked up, eyes half closed, his fingers on her clit again.

"Ah… Yes…" The lioness hissed. "Yes, Arne… Mmmph, just like that!"

He was close too, even though he didn't need to announce it – not until the point of orgasm when a blasting neigh broke from his lips and he pressed as much of his paw and fingers over her clit and pussy as possible, perhaps knowing that it was not a time for delicacy. He screamed his bareback triumph to the world at large and there was no denying that they had certainly annoyed others in adjoining hotel rooms, though Eda couldn't find it in herself to care. No, she didn't care, not one little bit, not as she grunted and heaved, shoulders rounding forward, lusting and longing for the moment more than she could ever have anticipated.

It was hers to take as white hot, blinding orgasm flashed before her eyes, her body rocking and grinding on his massive cock as if she was possessed. And perhaps Eda was, though it was only in the best of ways as his cum flowed up inside her, forcing her to accommodate it while the swell around his cock, inflating her softly with his seed, grew and grew and grew. As orgasm ripped through her and the lioness howled out her pleasure like a wild cat of the plains, the outline of the cock in her softened and eased away, replaced by a light bulge of cum, the equine's over productive orgasm needing to go somewhere.

It was just the first time, the first time of many together, yet it could not have gone more perfectly, the lioness panting over his chest while the stallion's balls ached and churned, spending every drop of cum that she could coax from his body.

Yes... She thought dimly. *Some things are just meant to be.*

In going for a ride, Eda might just have found more than what she had been looking for.

Bondage & Impregnation

"Oh, yeah, baby... Ohhhh!"

Luna cried out, the wolf arching her back, only her tail left free. Even the heavy, leather collar around her neck weighed her down, felt as if it was pinning her in place as her hips rocked.

Yet the wolf anthro with her pure white fur and long, silver hair was not free to do as she willed, not in any way, a raw hunger and "ferality" (she probably made that word up) coursing through her with every beat of her heart. She was sort of suspended, in a T-pose kind of cross, her folds dripping after so many orgasms that the wolf could barely see straight. Her arms spread out comfortably to either side of her body whereas her legs were spread, the bondage equipment well-padded and comfortable for long term play. At least, that was what her husband had told her it was for.

She hadn't been in the playroom before quite like that, not with Devon, but the tall, powerful stallion with a jet-black coat and white snip on his nose oozed power. He didn't have to tie her up, bringing his wife into her persona as his submissive, to take control, but it did help so very much. The stallion nickered throatily, his eyes dancing with dark glee, a hard, throbbing length of stallion meat already pushed from his sheath, firming up fully with the last few throbs of blood. The head was flat but not yet flared, offering a gleam of pre-cum as a temptation for what was yet to come.

"Little puppy," he crooned, his voice soft, suave, wrapping around her like warm velvet. "There's no need to struggle so... What is it that you seek, darling?"

The control that he had over her could not be denied in Devon's words, though Luna hissed through her teeth and howled even more readily for him. The damn stallion had had a vibrating massage wand on her fucking pussy for hours already, soaking her silly with orgasm after orgasm – and he had the *nerve* to ask her what she wanted from him?

The wolf howled, twisting her head back and forth, though the claiming pressure of the collar kept her from writhing too far, her hair a wild, silver mess. Fuck, how did the damn horse know how to get her riled up each time? To that extent, to the extent where she was a wild mess, no longer able to control herself, needing the heavy leather cuffs and secure chains of the bondage to keep her locked down to the tilted "cross" that she was positioned on... Hmmph... If she didn't love her husband so much – and want to be bred and fucked while she was raw with heat – she would have lain him out for daring to tease her so.

As it was, the situation called for it, her fur matted with sweat, need coursing through, beat after beat of her heart demanding that she dance to the tune of it.

"Just fucking put it in me!" She snarled, relishing in the bondage and wanting to be free of it simultaneously. "Fuck me silly – breed me!"

Sharp, snappy, far from sweet: that was how she was, how she yearned to be, empowered by her true self. She was too wild, too powerful, her claws sharp where other anthros had fingernails, her eyes darkening to a twisted amber that spoke of the times where their kind had been feral, wild, untamed. And so was Luna in that moment, heaving and panting, her breasts rolling with every dragged breath into her lungs, only the wagging of her tail betraying how she loved it so very much.

Forced? Not at all, not when her eyes were fixed on her husband's thick length, how he pumped it languidly with a paw, coming up close enough to rest between her legs, his cock on her abdomen rather than *in* her pussy.

"This…dearest of mine?"

She screamed, trying to hump her hips up, but there was even a leather band around her midriff, ensuring that she stayed right where her husband wanted her to be, grunting, heaving, lost in lust but still ready for breeding. There was nothing else she needed to be, not in that moment, mindless with passion, driven to so many orgasms that she should have been wiped out and yet…

…and yet she still craved more. She yearned for his cock, the sensation of being stretched out, the skin of his shaft moving lightly over his length as he sealed the full meat of his spire inside her pussy. But he made her whimper for it, beg for it, whining and panting, her body a mess with sweat and curled, damp fur, before he fed it to her.

"Ohhhhh!"

Inch by inch. Devon did not need words to dominate and to claim his wife, sliding into her, forcing her to feel every delectable inch of his cock stretching her out, pushing deeper, bit by bit. It was there for her, every last fibre of it, thick and wanton, her chest heaving, eyes glassy as she gasped through silent, shaking orgasm.

In that moment, she was his, completely and utterly, her heart and her soul held in his gentle paws, though his control was absolute. Her pussy rippled around him in orgasm, though the contractions and judders of the wolf's bound body were erratic, not something to be held in high acclaim, considering how needy she was. Yet the hot slop of her pussy soaked his dick as he eased into her.

The stallion could have taken her in a single thrust, slammed deep, used every inch of his cock to put her in her place, to show the wolf who was the one who held the reins between them. But he did not for it was more effective still to go slowly and easily, sliding into her, letting her feel how his half-formed flare scraped luxuriously against her inner walls, clasping him like warm velvet, however they dripped with her arousal.

Luna howled, her head thrown back as far as it could go, trying to twist back and forth, to rock under him, to do something, anything, yet all the wolf could do was to lie there and take it. Every slow, pounding, deliberate stroke from the equine, Devon driving into her, filling her with every stroke. There was not a single inch of his cock that was left outside her pussy, Devon smirking as he powered into her, straining her sex wide, the slickness of her dripping folds clasping him tightly.

"Unff..." She gasped, lips parted, her hair swiftly turning into a tangled mess. "Yes... Ohhhh, yes!"

It was deep and it was filling and it took every last bit of her bondage to hold her there, leather creaking, the bondage cross groaning under her attempts to thrash. Yet all Luna knew was the explosion of orgasm as the thick flare of his cock and the medial ring both dragged over her G-spot, taking her to highs that the wolf did not think possible after orgasming so many times already. The slick slop of his cock pushing into her filled the room, only overruled by her howls, her cries echoing off even the padded walls of the playroom.

Yet there was nowhere else that the wolf would rather have been, her whole body aching with need, even if she was getting everything she needed right there and then. His cock powered through her, driving up to her innermost barrier, giving her the impression that something was shifting inside her. It was an uncomfortable sensation, really, to have her cervix pushed like that, and yet it was such a primal, raw sensation that she could not help but crave it too.

The harshness of it. The desire of it. The snarl of power coursing through her. She needed it, so lustful that she had to be bound simply to be controlled, to be dominated, to be used as she so desperately needed. The craving of need was worse than she could ever have anticipated, howling, ripping, powerful need coursing through her body, her stomach churning, though part of that was the bulge of his cock showing through her lower abdomen. It was huge, so very thick that it forced its way through all the same, forcing her to submit, despite quivering, rippling delight teasing her form.

She had to soften to it, one way or another, the calling of new life deep within her begging to be allowed forth into the light. It had to come and she reclaimed a little more control over herself with every orgasm that wracked her form, his massive length of meat powering into her, deeper and deeper, even if there was nowhere else at all for it to go.

Still, she craved it, Devon's cocky smirk taking hold as he tipped forward over her, enjoying the moment, the lust of it all, grunting, moaning, her head spinning and swirling. She needed it and she was so lucky that the stallion was there to claim her, to breed her, though the enormity of what they were to do still blossomed through. She knew that their time there together would come out in something greater than both of them, taking them into a new chapter of their lives, but there was a better way to enjoy it too, the fetish of it pulsing through in every beat of her heart.

"Oh, yes... Fuck... Fuck me! Breed me!"

She snarled out her snapping cries as Devon held onto her, one paw curled around her shoulder and the other on her hip, though there was no need for the stallion to hold her in place. Yet the driving push of his hips demanded that she sacrifice even more to him, that she give up everything she was, everything she had. For it all had to come out in the delight of it all, in every snarl, in every driving pound of his hips slapping between her spread, raised thighs.

Fuck! She needed it, head dizzy, her body pulsing, aching, so much so that the wolf barely even realised that she was climaxing until it had swept over once again. Luna howled, head thrown back, though Devon was right there to hold her, squeezing her shoulder, driving into her with a hot, rampant slap of flesh on flesh.

Through her cries of lust, she saw him as she loved him the most, as if she had peeled back every layer of what made the stallion a stallion, who he was in himself, his mane a little wilder around his face, his cock plumping out inside her. The power of him was apparent in every tensing, bunching muscle, need coursing through, though she was there to take it, whimpering for him, even as his breath caught.

There was no stopping the splurge of his seed shooting up inside her, however, all that she lusted for in the thrill of mating, in breeding, in knowing that there was no going back from being seeded in the peak of fervour. He leaned over her, sharing breath, claiming her lips in a kiss, despite the threat of her sharp teeth. It was there that Luna claimed his moans as her own too, kissing him back hungrily, the stallion's hips still working, pushing on, all to spend every drop of thick, virile cum inside her pussy.

Every small thrust, every tiny grind of his hips… It all came down to that moment of heaving, sweaty lust, hips rocking, breath catching in shared passion. Devon's shaft flared inside her, giving the wolf that tiny extra stretch that even she could not have predicted.

It was better than she had imagined, shuddering lightly, her lower abdomen bloating out just a little from the sheer, thick volume of horse cum that Devon pumped up inside her. Her heart pounded for him, an ache deep inside yet to be fulfilled, yet he was there to hold her tightly, to let her know that everything was all right, that there was nothing at all that she had to worry about except being the best wolfess she wanted to be.

Luna shuddered, moaning in the afterglow. The throb of his cock inside her still pumped out drops of cum, Devon softening the kiss a touch, his lips moving with hers.

"I love you..."

He breathed, barely allowing her a moment to register what had been said, though she kissed him back with the fervour that she hoped told him just how she felt about him too, the desire in her heart. Love was permanent, at least for her, the depth of her bond with Devon... But she loved how he treated her in the bedroom just as much, indulging every last one of her kinky little desires so that she could, in fact, finally indulge in sexual satisfaction like no other.

Deep inside, his seed worked away, slipping deeper and deeper, seeking out her waiting womb. There was only one place for it to go, after all, one thing that could come from a rampant, bareback mating in the throes of heat...

And she couldn't wait to see her belly rise and swell in evidence of her fertility.

Everything was perfect, exactly the way it was. It didn't need to be anything more than what it was. Even if everything was going to change, bringing new life into their arms and another facet of their relationship to develop.

She shivered, whimpering softly into her husband's mouth.

She couldn't wait to see where they would go together.

Dystopian Passion

Werewolves & Vampires

"Ah... Oh, Lou... I... I don't think..."

But the werewolf blushed as his vampire lover playfully pinned him back against one of the many broken-down buildings in the city. There, finding a place that wasn't in a dystopian state of disrepair, though they said it "wasn't the apocalypse" was unlikely to happen – and if anyone did they were more likely than not to deface it in some way. There were more than enough bombs and items of destruction available on the black market and the open market those days, gang wars breaking out, taking over towns and cities, fighting for territory.

Such was the battle of living in a dystopia... Yet love too could be found there.

Lou smirked, the vampire fox grinning, fangs flashing in the dying rays of the sun. The werewolf with brown fur and a slightly hunched-over posture, Carson, was a good head and shoulders taller than her, though that had never bothered her in the slightest. It did not temper her playful control over him, though that was all soft in their relationship, something that did not come with the bitter bite of gang warfare.

But they were...in rival gangs. That posed a problem.

But not that evening, not as the sunset cast rich orange and crimson shades across the wreck of the city, her teeth nipping at his neck without drawing blood. Lou smirked, palming her paw down over the bulge of his crotch, watching how it rose to attention even through his ripped trousers, how they hung over his strong, muscled thighs. The red fox should not have been able to hold a candle to him physically, though the white tip of her tail and how it cut down from the underside of her jaw, dipping into her low neckline set off the bright hue of her fur in a way that nothing else ever could.

Carson shuddered, though he let her mount him, clinging to his shoulders, his back to the wall. A gun fell to his side, though it was only there, for him, for self-defence at a distance: something that werewolves were not all that good at, to be fair. Close-range combat was more their thing, but he would never utilise anything at all like that, not against her, never against her. He moaned as she kissed him, eagerly slipping his long, flexible tongue into her muzzle in turn, though he knew well enough what his illicit lover wanted.

Even though the fox was not of his gang...he didn't care. He was so sick to death of war and fighting and gangs that went up against one another without really knowing why they were doing it. Society had crumbled, though there were still ways to access technology, so much reserved for the obnoxiously rich that they had all been left behind.

But that was fine, a grunt rising in the back of his throat as his hard-on throbbed and ached. He held her tightly in his arms, even with Lou's legs wrapped around his waist, sweeping her down to the ground, only to fumble at freeing his erection. The fox stretched out deliciously, her crop top riding up even higher to expose more of her creamy white belly.

"I see you have a package for me, stud..." She all but purred. "Why don't you bring that down here and make me forget all about the last raid, huh?"

Carson barked a short laugh, a hot pole of wolf-flesh throbbing into his paw, stroking it lightly, though it had already pushed from his sheath to full attention. His balls were left tucked back inside his trousers and undergarments, though he was swift to help Lou out of her trousers too, the tightly fitted, stretchy fabric a pain in the arse to wrestle down off her legs, boots off and all.

Yet she allowed it, arching up to meet him when they were off and spreading her knees apart, welcoming him in against her and exposing the pink slit of her pussy. The werewolf growled, diving between her legs, though his tongue lashed out keenly, swiping over it, delving inside, drinking in her sweetness as if it was the only life-giving nectar that he would ever need again. Her moans carried softly, all to his ears and his ears alone, while he drove his tongue into her, curling it up against the spot where he knew her G-spot was.

There was no sense in not pleasing her, not when his heart beautifully brimmed over with adoration for her. Fuck the world, fuck the dystopia – all Carson ever wanted was to be in that moment with her, always and forever. Nothing else would make him happy or happier, for it was where he needed to be, her cream dancing on his tongue as he lapped deeply, scooping it into his muzzle with great thanks.

He whimpered against her, the fox's hips rising, grinding her pussy more and more urgently against his nose as if she too was losing control. Lou cursed under her breath, legs shaking, and he loved that he could draw on that for her, to make her feel as if she was slipping from some sense of reality too, the sense of control that, before, she had clung to so viciously.

"Oh... Yes... Yes, more... Carson..."

She breathed out his name as if it was a promise, but the werewolf needed more, so much more. They had their own powers and specialities, which was perhaps why they had survived as long as they had in a dystopian world, though there were others too that could do what they did. Lycans were powerful, yes, but so were vampires – and being able to sustain herself on blood and not merely food was what had gotten Lou to where she was.

The beauty of their coming together was not in the amusing yet typical rivalry of werewolf and vampire, not even as Lou took back control and pinned the wolf on his back, though his tail still wagged fervently, wanting more. No... It was in how they could use those things to come together, casting off the shrouds of demands and claims on them and their lives, finding passion despite all else.

"You make me want to ride you and fuck you all day," she growled, claws pricking into her chest where she leaned over him, straddling his hips with intent. "And I can keep you here too, if I want to..."

Carson smirked, paws on her hips, muscles bulging, though the werewolf knew better than to say anything back to her, most definitely so. No, he knew his place and if that was taking a light drop of submission under Lou, well...he was more than happy with that. Especially as her dripping pussy teased over the tapered head of his cock, sliding back and forth, letting it press inside her. And yet the fox vampire took him slowly, deeper and deeper, letting his dick slide succulently into her pussy, though she was the one well and truly in control.

It was the way of it for them, though Carson was more than happy with that, even if it was a strange kind of torture to be lying flat on the ground, the stone hard against his back, trying to thrust up into her pussy. And yet Lou controlled him as well as she always did, forcing him to bear through, taking more and more of his cock until she sank to the base and the knot that had not yet swollen, squeezing around him.

"Don't think about anything else, puppy," she murmured, eyes fixed on him, blue orbs burning with an intensity that took his breath away. "Just me. Eyes on me."

The world didn't matter, not when they were together, for it was not as if they could do anything about the state of the wider dystopia around them. Better to take what pleasures they could from the moment while they carved out their safe place in the world and worked out, later, what to do about themselves, their relationship, where their place was in it, in the end. Her pussy clenched around him and her werewolf whimpered, rocking up at her, though, sunk into a crouch, she could take as much or as little of him as she wanted.

And Lou wanted it all, rising and falling, fucking his shaft as he grunted and tried to rock up against her. But the werewolf had something for her, his fingers creeping around to the front of her pussy, not willing to let her pleasure go unnoticed. He pressed her clit lightly, letting her rock into his touch, circling it harder, letting her judge how much she could take and what she needed at any given time. It was harder for him to use a more delicate touch in such a position, but scooping up a little of the natural arousal from her pussy where it creamed around the join of their bodies helped slicken the path of his fingers.

As the werewolf rubbed her clit, Lou growled, pushing down harder, riding her lover in the dying rays of the sun like her life depended on it. Yes, more, more... She needed *more*! The light glanced off her sharp fangs, always a vampire and unable to hide it, but she didn't care, grinning widely as she slammed her hips down on him.

Slowly but surely, his knot plumped up inside her, swelling, and she ground down all the way, not willing to let a treat like that go. Carson squirmed and barked something about not wanting to tie this time with her, that it was too risky, but she didn't care, not when it was her body too that she was taking a risk with.

Bareback, yes, but breeding between a fox and a wolf was not all that common. It was unlikely at best...

Yet she still shivered at the *chance* as his knot inflated inside her, locking them together, grinding on it as her pleasure spiked sharply. That was what she'd needed, the aching pulse and strain of it against the entrance to her pussy, the swell visible in the thickness around her entrance, all the most sensitive nerve endings clustered in one place. Then and only then did Lou allow herself to go, rocked forward to balance on his chest with one hand as she let out a fox-like yowl of lust.

"Ah... Yes... Ohhhh!"

Orgasm exploded through her, though it was Carson who was yet to cum, panting heavily, a hot spill of pink tongue flowing from the werewolf's muzzle. He moaned, holding her tightly, claws digging lightly into her hips, though he needed it too, passion swamping him, even if adoration for his more dominant partner was, of course, the most prominent feeling. His cock throbbed inside her, his knot pulsating, and he knew that he could not hold off for very much longer at all, not as he groaned and grunted, lust locked up in his throat.

Yet the rampant humps and grinds of his partner against his knot could not help but pull him over the edge with her and he let out a long, drawn-out howl to match her yowl as he too let go in dystopian passion. He needed it, ached for it, spending rope after rope of hot, virile cream into her bare pussy – but only time would come to tell the tale of that risky liaison.

In dystopian passion, humping and grinding as the sun faded below the horizon, no one there to bear witness to their illicit tryst but them, they had one another. And that was everything that they needed, groaning deeply, rocking together, all until Lou slumped over Carson's chest, the broadness of it drawing her down, cradling her. Even though she was very much strong enough to not need to be cradled and held like that, it was still good, of course, to have a partner that she could trust in that way.

Everyone needed that. Even if they did not say it aloud.

In dystopian passion, even a werewolf and a vampire from rival gangs could come together, finding solace in a world that was never made for them.

As they kissed, they knew they'd always have one another.

And that was okay too.

Study Break

Gloria grinned, the dragoness leaning back on the bed, her tail hanging off the edge of it, swinging back and forth lazily. With a fluffy tip to it, t was far from the most menacing of tails, though Gloria had never, quite honestly, wanted to be a menacing kind of dragon. She was softer and fluffier and unlike some dragons that she had seen about the mixed-anthro university campus and town beyond, she had skin rather than scales. It was a lot softer and sweeter than anything that a scaled dragon could boast, but the pale blue skin and the richer blue hue of her mane of hair and her tail-tuft were unique to her and Gloria would always love that.

She loved her partner even more. Never before had Gloria thought that she would fall for anyone as hard as she had fallen for Graeme, another dragon at the university, though he was studying anthro history specifically, rather than delving into magic studies like her. She licked her lips more softly, gazing at him through half-lidded eyes, smoky breath curling around her nostrils.

The small university bedroom was set into a dorm where there were several bedrooms all leading off a shared hallway, every anthro getting their own separate bedroom, which was something at least. Gloria had looked, before, at studying abroad, but there were a lot of places over there where shared rooms were the norm and she had never slept in the same room as anyone else, bar at a sleepover, when she'd been younger. It had been hard enough or her to get used to sleeping in bed, occasionally, with Graeme, her boyfriend, and there was barely enough space there for them anyway. Still, it was worth getting used to having another warm body against hers, for all the joy that he brought her and the challenges too. He was the first guy, let alone a dragon, that she had slept with and there would always be that connection between them.

Still, her eyes swept over his grey-scaled form, sitting at the desk while she sprawled out on the bed, his hair a tuft of brown, though it seemed small between his large horns. Sometimes, Gloria had wondered if they were particularly heavy for him or made him knock his head on doorframes, but Graeme had always been lightly considerate of the space that he took up and anything around him, even furniture. His tail hung loosely over the back of the swivelling computer chair, his laptop open in front of him. Her eyes, however, were not in work, not as something built and built between her legs, warming her through. Gloria nipped at her lip, if only to hide away her smirk for just a little bit longer.

The hour was late and they were studying... But wherever would the fun have been in studying without any kind of study break, hm? Oh, she didn't see the point in that, not at all, ahead on her classes, even ifs he'd wanted to study with Graeme too, all so she could do her little bit to support him. She was larger than him, easily by about a head, though his body was smaller and slighter than her curves, a slim, educated sort of dragon who preferred using other means of transport to get around than his legs or wings. Although Gloria did not often fly, she'd gotten rather into ball sports at the university, just for the fun of it.

"Graeme..." She breathed, her sweet, almost lavender-scented smoke curling around her nostrils, pouring a little of her magic into her smoke, not wanting to release fire in the small confines of Graeme's room. "Why don't you come over here and keep me company for a bit?"

"Hm?"

He blinked and looked up, dazed as if she had caught him in a real moment of concentration. Gloria grinned, sitting up on the bed, stretching her arms out over her head. Even though he was not expecting that kind of attention from her, he blinked and sat up a little straighter. Even though he was someone who tried to be as focused and as studious as possible, Graeme could not be faulted at all for still being a drake, his eyes dropping to her chest. Just as Gloria wanted...

"Hey..." She purred, her tail curling back and forth, toying with his attention and drawing his eye even further downwards. "Don't you want to spend some time with me instead, darling?"

Graeme squirmed, tail tucked down, clearly torn.

"I do..." He said slowly, as if he was dredging the words up. "But... Oh, Gloria... Mmm... You make it so hard to study, sometimes, I know... But I really have to ace this test..."

It was not an important test. Gloria knew that, only one that was a benchmark of how far the class had come during the semester, though there would be exams at the end of it, usually one or two for each class. They were fortunate to not have too intense of a workload when a lot of their respective studies came under the heading of coursework, though it was a different kind of intensity and personal study that they both had to undertake.

If it was important, genuinely and sincerely, the dragoness would never have done what she did next. Slipping down to her knees, she crawled over the carpet, crossing the very short distance between them as her boyfriend stared, wide-eyed, a soft moan on his lips. She made sure to present herself at her most sensual – which, for Gloria, most often meant simply relaxing and being herself, which suited her just fine.

She only wanted to be herself, anyway, regardless of what teasing sexual delights she was trying to take for. Licking her lips, she made sure her curves were on full show, her shorts feeling like they were barely covering her arse as she crawled, lifting her tail a bit more so that they were tugged up even higher than before. Her breasts were large and full, considerable for her form, though Gloria still thought that they suited her broader shoulders well. She was not a soft, delicate sort of dragoness, despite the smoothness of her skin, blowing a stray strand of her light blue mane from her face.

"I'll take care of you, darling..." She murmured. "You can keep on studying, don't let me get in your way."

Of course, Gloria would never truly get in his way, not at all, even though he could not have said anything. Graeme could have stopped her if he really wanted her to, but, truly, the dragons didn't want to call halt to what had been started between them.

"Mmmph..."

He groaned, tail twitching back and forth, though she did not miss how his lips twitched in a smile, as if Graeme was trying to hide, even from her, what he truly wanted. She ran her fingers up his legs, parting his thighs to slide between them, her tongue hanging out to drag against her lips as she moaned softly, leaning in closer and closer.

"The spark of magic always gets my blood hot," she murmured, rolling her hips back as if she was already imagining her partner thrusting into her, filling her pussy with his meat. "I need you... And I've been wanting to taste you since my last magic practice session ended..."

He made a strangled little sound in the back of his throat, eyes wide with desire that he was barely even able to hold back.

"Unff... Gloria..."

"Shush now," she breathed. "Let me take care of you. Tell me if you want more of something, less of something, something else... Otherwise, just let me take care of your every need and everything's going to be okay, darling..."

She breathed out his name, a whisper on her lips, unzipping his jeans and smirking when Graeme, very obligingly, lifted his hips at the same time to allow her to slide down his jeans, just a little b t. They could not have been the most comfortable thing for him to wear for studying, but he hadn't wanted tc get as comfy as she was, even if she would have that side of him out in time. Graeme deserved, of course, to be comfortable around her, even more so when she freed his erection from his underwear and jeans, the hard length of grey-skinned dragon cock springing up as if it had only been waiting all along for her attention and hers alone.

She liked to think like that, sliding her hand along his cock, down to the base, to pull the skin along his uncut shaft, showing the pink of the head. It was most often tucked away within his skin, for he was all natural and all dragon, but she leaned in too quickly to lap and tease over the sensitive cock tip with her tongue.

"Ohhhh..."

Bolstered by his moans, she lapped more eagerly, her tongue sliding over the curiously slick flesh, which always came with a very smooth feel to it, even if the flesh softened and yielded light y even under the touch of her tongue. He was fully swollen there, throbbing in her touch, though she left his balls tucked back away in his underwear. She didn't need to get them out into the cool air, not yet, for what she had in mind, patiently lowering her head, taking his cock into her mouth.

"Oh, fuck..."

Ah, she loved when she could get Graeme to swear like that. He was usually so quiet and reserved, but she'd fallen in love with those subtler, softer sides of him. Still, well and truly letting the dragon out was something that she enjoyed too, letting him express himself and letting Graeme know that he never, ever, would have to hold anything back around her.

She took him deep into her maw, cradling him on her tongue, even though her tongue was quite narrow, almost forked – but she had not inherited that gene from her mother. It was tapered at the tip with a thicker, rounder head, but fleshy enough too that she could skilfully hook it around his cock, sliding it down and around the base even as she sucked him. The drake didn't have a sheath, not like some anthros, but she leaned into him, imagining that she was trying to get her nose all the way down to his crotch and lower abdomen, sucking him hard in the tight pressure of her lips.

"Ah!"

Graeme's hips thrust and bucked and his hands, trembling, came down on her head, as if they were searching for horns to grab. There were no horns, not for her, so he had to avoid her larger ears, which twitched back and forth to catch every sound, her mane and forelock spilling neatly between them from where she kept it exceptionally well-brushed. There was no one quite like Gloria to take care of their personal needs, after all, and Gloria relaxed into giving him head, purring softly around his shaft.

There was time there, more than enough time for her to savour every little moment, every little twitch of his flesh, how the muscles in Graeme's thighs tightened when he was trying to hold back just a little bit more. He grunted faintly, smoke curling from his nostrils, though she had never seen him breathe fire before, not yet. That was okay, very much okay, as she rested her hands on his thighs and trusted her maw to do the work for her, twining and twisting her long, flexible tongue wetly around his cock.

"Mmmph…"

It was a tight fit to suck him off, even for her, considering that a dragon's muzzle was often longer and shaped well for such pleasures. Her nose twitched, eyes closing, losing herself there, in the throb of soft flesh on her tongue, how he was firm but not so much so that he did not "give" a little when she closed her lips even more firmly around him. Gloria tried to suck hard enough that her cheeks hollowed, but that was not the kind of pressure that Graeme enjoyed and she backed off from it, bobbing her head moderately, teasing him but not going so quickly that she was going to bring him off in a few moments.

No… Oh, no. She wanted him to enjoy everything, every moment, drawing it out and out and out for him, bit by bit, moment by moment. She grunted, hips rocking, though the heat between her legs would have to be satisfied at another time, her hand wanting to go down there but not trusting herself to give Graeme her full attention otherwise.

And that was the kind of dragoness she was. She didn't do anything by halves and she committed fully to everything that she did, even when that came down to something as simple as sucking dick. She gave everything to him, soothing away the stresses of the day and studying, even though, of course, Graeme wasn't at all interested in studying anymore. It would have been hard for him to study, after all, when his cock was in the warm grasp of a dragoness' maw, but that didn't matter, no, not all that much.

Not when she was there to take care of him, knowing truly that her needs too would be taken care of later. He never left her wanting and most certainly never left her waiting. She just wanted to give back to him too, always making sure that he had his fill. Or else Graeme was the kind of dragon to forget about his own needs entirely and, with Gloria, that simply would not do…

Slowly but surely, the dragoness had begun to take more and more of the lead in their sexual adventures together, though she bobbed her head faintly, savouring his cock, the thought and the notion only in the back of her head. She wasn't focusing on it, not when she had a firm rod of shaft begging her attention, but it was there, encouraging her, driving her on to find the true nature of her sexuality and everything that sang to her and her heart alone. Maybe she was a little more dominant and caregiving too than she'd realised, though Graeme would help her explore all that inside her, all in good time. She would never have expected anything less from the drake that she adored with all her heart, sucking down his cock into the back of her throat with ruthless intent.

"Mmph! Gloria… I'm…"

He was sensitive, so very sensitive, and getting close too. Her neck ached a little and the carpet was rough on her bare knees, though that was nowhere near enough to get the dragoness to stop, not when she had gotten going. No, she wanted the treat of his cock, every drop of his cum flowing down her throat, letting her savour it, relish in it, eyes closed, sensation and scent her driving forces. Unconsciously, Gloria's tail curled around and latched itself around his ankle, holding the drake in place even though Graeme, most certainly, wasn't going anywhere.

She "glacked" quietly around his cock, pushing a little too hard against her gag reflex, the computer chair squeaking as he adjusted his weight, shifting with need. He needed her, so much, and Gloria was there to give everything to him, his hands on her head reassuring and steadying even as she sucked him down. Taking the head into the back of her throat, she let the natural pressure of her gulping and swallowing take him deeper and deeper, stimulating and caressing him as he grunted and tipped forward.

"Ah... Oh... Ohhh..."

So close – but not quite. For it was Gloria that pushed him over the edge, moaning around his cock as he hunched over her and climaxed hard, spending thick ropes of cum into her maw. There was more seed there than usual and she dimly wondered if it had maybe been a bit longer since they had last fucked, but, well, she'd have to make sure that that didn't happen again. Not that having a bit of time where she was really able to drink down every throbbing spurt of a thicker, even creamier load than usual was not a bad thing either.

No... Gloria took everything that he gave her and more, keeping up the soft, sucking pressure around his cock, her tongue flickering and sliding back and forth erratically. He didn't know where her tongue was going to come from next or what she was going to do, rocking forward in pleasure upon pleasure, balls giving all that they had to give.

As the thrusts slowed, warm cum sliding sensually down her throat, the dragoness murmured around his cock, drawing back only so that she could clean him off, leaving his cock slick with her saliva, though that was fine by both of them. They could shower off soon enough, enjoying the closeness of their bodies pressed up to one another, but the moment was just for them, the warmth of Graeme seeping through his scales into her, her eyes opening to take him in, his fingers combing through the softness of her hair.

And she held him there, lashing off and cleaning even the too-sensitive tip of his cock, until he couldn't bear it anymore. With the head of his cock glistening with saliva and the tiniest pearl of cum, he half slumped back in the squeaky chair, the wheels scooting him back just a little. Yet Gloria went with him, purring, licking her lips, making sure that not a single tiny drop of his seed was wasted. For there was far more for the dragons to experience together and they had to see it all through for themselves, lust rising, passion mounting, tangling together in the deviousness of the moment.

She would have her fill, once he'd caught his breath, smoke curling softly from her nostrils once more. But, right then, all that she needed was him and his fingers brushing through her hair, letting her know that he was there, need rising, her own yet to be sated.

It may have been dark outside, but, as students of the university, they still had so much more fun to take while others were off partying and doing their thing.

In his hall room, the dragons found that they had plenty more to occupy their attention as their study break grew longer and longer and longer…

Breeding the Librarian

The Wolf and the Bunny

"Oh, Arlo..."

The wolf growled, pressing in close to the librarian bunny, pinning her arms up above her head against the bookcase. Diana arched up against him, thrusting her hips passionately forward, the skirt that she was wearing surely too short for work. It was not as if the library had much of a dress code, especially at the university, but there was still some set requirement there, surely, about not wearing things that were too revealing. Of course, her glasses were still perched on her nose, slipping a little, but the wolf thought that only added to the look she was going for.

Not that Arlo minded at all, the grey wolf nuzzling into her neck, Diana's lips parting in a breathy moan that was far too quiet for the peaceful shelving. The bunny's ears flopped back softly, tan and white, her fur beautifully groomed. He could not help, quite clearly, nuzzling into it, nipping at her neck, his sharp teeth catching and pulling.

Diana breathed out against him, her blue eyes intense. Her small pink tongue flicked out against her lips, though Arlo silenced her cry in a kiss, his long, powerful tongue winding around hers and sweeping back.

He deepened the kiss as he bore her back, though her hind paws still scrabbled against the floor in her heels. They were four inches high, give or take, and a biting, shocking red, the kind of red that should have been seen out clubbing or dancing, not in the university library.

The wolf growled into the kiss as Diana, once again, bucked up against his hard-on. Oh, they knew that there was only so much time they had there, so much they could do, not wanting to get caught, but the sweetness between them still had to be fed, one way or the other. And it wouldn't have been as fun for either of them if Arlo had done something like sneak her back to his room.

He thought she might have had a husband, but, honestly, he didn't know, or care, one way or another. Sometimes the bunny was wearing a ring and sometimes she wasn't, so the wolf more than felt that he was free to make his own decision on that one.

She kissed him back passionately, however, and moaned his name, all to the point that the wolf felt confident in taking her, releasing her paws, letting her fumble down with the light belt he had slipped through the loops of his jeans. Diana smirked cheekily, making quick work of it, glancing down the line of shelves as if she heard someone coming. Arlo groaned.

"Fuck, Diana, what are you doing to me?"

She grinned and blew him a kiss, her skirt sliding up to reveal a little more of her thigh. From where the wolf's paw had gone earlier, however, he already knew that she was not wearing any underwear, if she had even started the day wearing any at all.

"Anything you want, pet…"

Arlo groaned, but didn't get a chance to do more as the bunny tugged his erection free of his jeans and underwear, sliding his clothing down just enough to free his shaft. His balls, however, had to remain tucked back in his boxer briefs, kept out of sight, for there was only so much time that they had there.

Maybe it was that risk that they enjoyed the most, how it strung out the heat between them to such an extent that they felt like they were going to burn up from the inside out if they did not find a way, some way, to quench the fire. It was that very heat that pooled in the pit of Diana's stomach as she let out a soft whine and squeak, fondling his cock as her lips brushed the tip, parting in a far more intimate kiss.

Arlo's paw smacked heavily into the bookshelf above her as she sucked down his cock, showing him exactly what bunnies were supposedly famous for. The wolf had not thought that that had been a thing beforehand, but, damn if Diana didn't want to show him everything her mouth and pussy could do! She groped his nuts through his jeans, rubbing and teasing lightly through the material, lips slurping down, caressing his cock in a tight seal that made him feel more than a little giddy and faint.

His other paw came down and caressed her long, brown hair, pulling out the light curls from it as he twisted his fingers into it. The bunny leaned into his grasp as if she was encouraging him to hold and pull her hair, though he didn't honestly know enough about Diana to understand if that was what she meant. He wouldn't hurt her, of course, one way or the other, but he knew that he wanted her, that he yearned for her, that what lay between them could have been fleeting or could have been long-lasting.

Only time would tell that. And he was keen to find out, grunting in the back of his throat as he powered into her mouth, letting her swallow down his cock, gulping around him as soon as he pressed into the back of her throat.

"Oh, fuck," he growled lowly, as quietly as he could. "That's the stuff..."

If anyone else, the other students at the university, knew what he was getting from the sweet librarian, they most likely would have not believed him – or else been sickeningly jealous of him. Not that Arlo cared, a bit of a lone wolf naturally, though that would have been just like his species. They were either born with a pack mentality or wanting to be out on their own, with some nuances in-between.

But what Arlo really wanted was to be with someone, to thrust and grind, to let the roll of his hips thrust his cock deep, sliding over her delicious tongue, adoring just how it flickered over and around the head of his cock. It was just something, something small, but it was still a connection with a partner and that was all, sometimes, that was needed.

She sank into the moment, taking him deep, swallowing down his thick cock. It had to be eight inches long and surely a little more to come at the base as she tenderly pushed his sheath back, bringing the owl to full, throbbing hardness as the tapered head of his cock pushed a little deeper still. The slick pre-cum trembling down her throat had her groaning, pressing into it more urgently, though she longed for more.

Arlo was a good lover, the sweetness of their quick, seductive liaisons, times together that no one else knew about, all the hotter for the tenacity of them. But the heat between her legs had been pooling there for quite some time already, letting her know that she was in need. Anthros could still come into heat, but it was something, for them, that was mostly managed by taking a few pills from the pharmacy, just to take the edge off it. It was a time, however, when they were more fertile. And maybe that had been exactly why Diana had dragged her favourite wolf out behind the deepest of the shelves, just to see if she could get a little relief.

The edge and the worry of being caught, however, was something that she was liking more and more. Almost more than the throbbing of his cock in her mouth, playing her tongue over the more sensitive tip just to hear him swallow a curse and shudder, squirming as he tried not to ram too far down her throat. She loved that he could contain himself, even in a moment like that, need coursing through, pump after pump of his cock driving him into a frenzy.

She taunted him, almost, the tip of her tongue flicking ardently over the tip of his cock until he grabbed her hair and dragged her all the way down. Her paw pressed between her legs as Diana tried to hold herself back, remembering that she didn't have her bag with her there and, besides, she didn't even know if there had been a condom in there anyway. Maybe the wolf had one… if not, their time together was going to be rather short-lived and more than a little frustrating. She didn't know if she could be quiet enough with the wolf's muzzle between her legs with his tongue lashing.

And what Diana really craved was to feel the burning head of his aching, beautiful hard-on ramming up inside her, hard and fast, claiming her as she so desperately wanted to be claimed.

That was her heat talking, but, well, it was still a need and still understandable, just like everything else.

The wolf, however, didn't seem to want to hold back either and her heart leapt as he withdrew from her mouth, loosening his grip on her mussed-up hair.

"Fuck, Diana, I want you so bad right now…"

"Then take me!"

He growled. Then he would do just that! Things didn't have to be difficult, not even for him, not even when he was in his university library and understood, in a way, that a lot was going on, that there were things that could have had him tossed out of university. He was risking a lot, just to get some pussy, though Arlo was not even sure that the bunny was more than that to him – or if she ever would be.

For them, it was all about the moment. Like the slide of his paw up her thigh as she stood, pushing against him, grunting, her eyes locking onto him with an intensity that had him gasping. She kissed him lightly, all in a way that made him want to press into it, though Arlo followed his instinct, hitching her up in his arms as she clung to him.

Her skirt hitched up as he pressed between them, pinning her against the bookcase as she closed her legs around his waist and hips, making sure that she would not fall.

Yet there was something there, as the bare head of his cock pressed up against her pussy, that they had not yet addressed.

Diana's half-closed eyes fluttered back open, lips parted as the wolf rolled suggestively against her, smearing his cock through her arousal, the folds of her pussy already slick with her essence. As if she could be anything but wet after everything, so far that day, that they had done together.

"Arlo…" She breathed, eyes locked with his as her legs tightened around his waist, keeping him there, his cock poised at the lips of her pussy. "I don't have a condom with me…do you?"

He froze, breath catching, a low, rumbling growl pulling from his lips.

"I don't care…" Oh, it was throwing caution to the wind, but he had to satisfy his need one way or the other and the horny part of him didn't care, not right then. "Do you? I will stop…"

Of course, he would. He would never have done anything, not at all, against her will. But the bunny moaned her acceptance and, with his agreement, sank onto his cock. All it took was a loosening of her paws where they clutched his shoulders, letting his shaft push into her. Arlo's breath caught and he kissed her deeply, longing for that moment, that surge of heat inside him.

Yet there was nothing quite like sinking into her – bareback at that! He'd never been inside the bunny bare before, but, well... Oh, he'd never want anything else after that. He knew it was a risk, but the wolf still thought, dimly in the back of his mind, that he could pull out, that he would have the self-control to do so. And there was always an emergency pill that he could get for her, if he couldn't pull out...

Back-ups resided in the back of his mind, but the wolf couldn't think about anything else as he speared into her, her velvety heat closing around his cock, massaging his length as if Diana was trying to take something from him. Yet all the bunny wanted was his cream, his load, everything that he had to give her spilling deep. It would sate her heat and take the edge off what she had been craving for so long, though it was not as if either of them were thinking straight in a moment like that.

It was all about the moment, the heat tangling between them as he groaned and powered into her, letting Diana balance herself against him, her grip tighter and tighter around him with every passing second. She squeezed him so hard that the pinch of heels, one shoe kicked off, almost gave him pause, but he couldn't stop his thrusting as he grunted and let her tuck her nose into the crook of his neck.

It was a strange sort of moment, her glasses sliding almost off the end of her nose, but it was what they needed, a little too intimate for what they had expected. But sometimes things could go places that they were never intended to and that was a fair thing, a good thing, a thing that they could take forward.

Or not. Either way, it was up to the bunny and the wolf exactly what they did, how they played it, lust and longing for that connection coursing between them. Arlo groaned deep in the back of his throat, trying to be as quiet as possible, though he rather thought that he was failing. As he sank deeper and deeper into arousal, he shook his head, nose tucking down, pulling her even closer in against his chest. The bookcase to her back at least gave them both something to support themselves on, though the knocking of their bodies against it shuffled the books, even knocking a couple off. Arlo put that down to them not being shelved properly, yet reminded himself in the same thought that he would need to make sure that there was no evidence left behind of their liaison.

For the end was coming, that lustful high, the pinnacle of climax. The wolf could feel it in how Diana closed around him, her pussy erratically twitching around his cock, trying to milk him of his load. And he knew he had to give it to her, one way or the other, slamming in hard and fast as the knot at the base of his cock swelled.

Diana snatched up his lips fiercely, forgetting their concern over him plunging into her, his knot swelling, pressing against her lips. It just felt too good to have him inside her without the barrier of a condom that she threw all caution to the wind, swept up and away in his arms and wanting nothing more than for the wolf to take her. Tongues of heat licked through her as she rolled her hips desperately against Arlo, though it was all up to the wolf to claim her, to show her all that he needed from her too.

He growled into her mouth, kissing her back deeply, though the kiss, at the very least, had the extra benefit of sealing away their cries, even if they were less in touch with their surroundings. Anyone could have walked up on them as her skirt fell around their crotches, half shielding what was happening between them, though they didn't care. Not as his knot locked them together, fully swelling inside her without either of them being of aware mind enough to pull back or out.

He howled into her mouth, the sound still managing to carry dully through the library, despite the deep kiss. His cock throbbed – but it was Diana who tumbled over the edge first, eyes closing, her ears softening down against the back of her head as she climaxed on his cock. She must have been worked up to lose control like that, but Arlo did not care, not even as the heat within rushed to his nuts, the ache in the base of his abdomen swelling.

He knew it was too much, that they had gone too far, but that thought was too easily overwhelmed by pleasure as he exulted in it, only able to thrust a little now that his knot stopped him from pulling out all the way. And yet every rope of cum that painted her pussy as he took his pleasure came with a throb of lust to it that had the wolf grunting into her muzzle, ears splaying out, his tail wagging faintly as his jeans slipped down a little further.

Thinking straight was out of the question as he grunted, leaning into her, his knot bulging, so thick, so tender, too sensitive at the point of pleasure, but there was nothing he could do about it then. He could only enjoy it, deepening the kiss, caressing her face with one hand, the other down on her buttock, helping her stay hitched up against him, her body as close to his as it was possible to be.

Diana whimpered, losing herself, dazed at the point of climax, though she was aware of the throbbing slosh of hot wolf cum trickling around his cock. Yet it had nowhere to go, not with his knot plugging her full, forcing her pussy to accept every last drop that he had given her. And there was no going back from that point, no wishing that they had taken further precautions, not when all was said and done and the heat of his aching member pulsated within her passage.

Arlo broke the kiss softly, leaning his forehead against hers, breathing her name.

"Diana..."

"Oh, Arlo."

Diana grinned, shaking her head at their folly, though it would all seem a lot less funny to her when the positive pregnancy test came up in the following weeks...

But perhaps that was all to be expected, when breeding a bunny.

Breeding the Leopardess

Exposed in Lust

It was a moment unlike any other, warming passion on the balcony of their holiday home in the South-West of England. The small apartment was cosy, but tucked around the back of the block in such a way that they had complete and utter privacy out there. The spring air cut crisply through them, salt and the freshness of the Cornish countryside winding around them, though the snow leopardess on her back with her legs spread for the big, spotted snow leopard wasn't thinking about that. No... Not as Evie lay back on the soft cushions that, not all that long ago, had been propped up on the chairs for the little balcony, the patio furniture that had been so graciously gifted to them. She purred up at her lover, her body bare but for her natural, tawny fur, though, unlike some anthros, Evie had a full head of hair too, her brunette locks spilling down from her head in a curly, glossy fall.

Sometimes that meant that she was mistaken for a male lion, for it looked somewhat like she had a mane, particularly when the curls did not behave and frizzed up a little. Even with her spots... Which could be annoying. But how could that at all be something that Evie worried about when her lover was there with her, his throaty purrs joining hers as he nuzzled into the crook of her neck. They were both snow leopards with silvery fur and black spots, white markings fluffy and light, though Darren was darker than she was. He even had some lion heritage, somewhere, in his lineage, a thicker ruff of black fur, like the mane of a lion, around his neck.

Darren growled playfully, though the leopard nudged her legs open a little more with his, easily dominating her. For them, it was not even the sort of thing that had to be vocalised, not after their years together, finding the rhythms and the nuances of lust and love entwined.

"My beautiful leopardess..."

Oh, how his rumbling purr washed over her... Their balcony looked out over the ocean and the coastline, but there was only so much that could be seen with the sun setting, casting a dim, pink haze over the ocean and the crashing waves lapping at the cliffs below. Darren nuzzled down her chest, kissing each breast, though Evie's body arched to meet up with his, pushing her chest up as if it knew that even more attention was coming.

"Yes... Darren..."

Every kiss electrified her, her hips rising, trying to press in close to him, but the leopard was already there, his thicker, darker mane framing his face, tail lashing back and forth in that eager feline fashion. Evie's breath caught and yet she froze there, sprawled out under his icy, dominating gaze, even if the quirk of her lover's lips softened his expression.

He did not have to be harsh, after all, when she was his lover, even if her eyes raked over his body, the rippling bulge of muscles. His black fur was sleek, laying over his muscles, though anthros with fur would very often find that the fur that they bore softened the edges of their muscles. If he had been merely scaled, perhaps, Darren would have appeared even more muscular than he was.

As it was, Evie bit her lip to quiet herself, just in case there was anyone else out on any of the other balconies, a low groan rising behind her lips. Oh, how she wanted to let it out, though that might have been too much, could have been too much, even if she knew that Darren would always protect her from any harsh words and shield her, always, from any manner of prying eyes.

His muzzle, however, slipping down between her thighs, was the sweetest thing of all, and she pushed up eagerly to meet him as his long, raspy tongue dipped up against her pussy, stroking her folds. It flicked back and forth, teasing her sex, and yet she ached for more, needed so much more, grunting and panting and moaning.

Tingles of heat, her heat, flowed through Evie, though it had been a while since a heat that potent had been upon her. Some anthros felt it as an aching need, a push for sex and an increase in their drive, but, to her, it felt like red-hot fire was lacing her veins, as if a dragon had taken up residence inside her and was breathing liquid flame into her body, following the network of her veins. Her claws extended as his tongue flickered up into her pussy and Evie desperately dug them into his mane. She just needed something to grip onto where she wouldn't hurt him, though the leopardess was sure too that Darren would not have minded one bit if she pricked him even with her sharp claws. Small things like that, momentary, passing bites of strain, simply didn't matter to them.

Maybe they even added to the moment.

"Oh... Darren, yes..." She moaned, letting her words fly free. "Yes... Deeper... Ohhh..."

Not even Evie could hide her groans forever, not when his tongue was doing such wonderful things to her, dragging out against her clit with every stroke. He was not rushed, not at all, but her skin prickled with need, aching for him more than ever. Didn't he know that she was in heat? Why didn't Darren want to fuck and breed her as much as she wanted him?

And yet he was the kind of dominant that was in control of himself too, warming and protective, his grey eyes flicking back up to her along the length of her tawny body. Evie knew that her curly hair was messier than she would have liked it to be, but it ceased to matter as his tongue curled around her clit, lapping and teasing, flicking back and forth over the sensitive little nub of flesh that, time after time again, had brought her so much pleasure from his desire. She panted heavily, her tongue lashing out over her dark lips, though there was nothing that the leopardess could do to ease things in the heat of the moment, only follow that sweet, sweet path towards orgasm.

There was nowhere else for her to go, not even as that cord of need strung taut within her, legs trembling, trying to keep them bent at the knee but weaker than she would have liked. Every fibre of her being screamed at her to collapse right then and there, to let him take her, to let him mount her, to let him fuck her, but she was fortunate that her big, strong leopard lover was right there to take care of her. Even if the very nature of that meant that she had to succumb, had to submit, had to give in to his wants, even if it might well have meant that she wasn't going to get what she wanted right away.

But that was okay... Evie shuddered bodily, languishing in freedom, even as Darren worked her up more and more, his paws under her backside, holding her gently up for the pleasure of his mouth. He would get her there, yes, sooner or later, definitely, one way or the other.

"Darren..." Even her voice, her words, was breathy, rasping lightly over her lips as if it was taking an awful lot more effort than usual to get them out. "I want... Oh... You... So...much..."

It didn't even sound like the leopardess' voice leaping from her lips, though there was only so much that she could do about that, especially when she had neither any desire nor any need to change it. She was his, always and forever, Darren chuckling against her cunny as he brought her right to the very edge of a tingling, aching orgasm, right there in the open air, and backed off once again. Evie groaned, hunger rather than frustration building. Darren had always known just how to toe the line there, even if there had been other more lustful notes in their relationships that had had to be adjusted to suit the both of them. That was the beauty of getting to know a partner in intimacy.

"My sweet..." He rumbled, kissing her inner thighs, all dark and dominant, tail lashing softly back and forth as if he was stalking the kind of prey that had already been caught. "Do you offer yourself to me?"

It was almost as if he was roleplaying with her, though Evie knew that he meant that far more seriously than even she could have imagined, that he wanted to make sure that she consented to it, that they both knew that his cock pressing up deep inside her, bare, meant. There was no going back from breeding bareback in heat, after all, even if it had been Evie, originally who had suggested that to him.

"Yes..." She breathed, letting him press her thighs down as he moved over her in a mating press, using his legs to keep hers pinned down and apart. "Yes, Darren... Yes, I want you, I want you... I want *all* of you."

Darren purred, pressing a kiss to her palm as she stroked his face, running her paws down the strong line of his jaw to his neck and shoulders as the leopard swiftly removed his boxer briefs. It was enough, more than enough, for them, always for them. For they had to be clear in their breeding intent beneath the setting sun, the crimson glow of it aching to orange at the close of the day. The tip of his cock pressed to her folds, ever so lightly teasing back and forth, as if he was not actually going to penetrate her.

Of course, he always would, for that was what his leopardess craved. He was not there to deny her, not at all, not as he rubbed back and forth, coating the tip of his barbed cock with her essence. Even though his ancestors had had rather hard, sharp barbs on their members, it was different for anthros, the barbs having softened over many, many years, though they were still designed to softly stimulate a partner. They were chunkier and plumped up with blood more softly than they would have been in the past and Evie groaned, arching up against him as if she was called there by a higher power, licking her lips, trying to find something, anything, through which she could distract her attention while need longed through her.

"Please... Darren... Breed me..."

It was all that he had been waiting for as the head of his cock pressed up to her aching, tender, plump folds. Blood had rushed to them, during his oral attention, and she yowled as they were further stimulated, her claws digging into his mane as his head pushed back down close to hers.

"My leopardess..."

It was with that deep, rumbling growl that he pushed into her at long last, Evie rocking and trying to arch up against him, but finding that she was completely pinned under his body and the mating press. The weight of his body over her was not something that she at all wanted to fight, the heat of him seeping into her body, though she still grunted and moaned, letting him penetrate her. Thrust after thrust bore through her body as she clung to him, needing, somehow, that ripping sense of stability in a moment that, otherwise, threatened to tear her away from the kind of reality that, even then, she found that she so very sorely needed to cling onto.

She needed him, ached for him, only for him, always for him.

Darren rumbled above her as he bred her, thrust after thrust powering into her pussy, barbs raking and pulling in just the right way. She yowled out his name, no longer even thinking about whether anyone else could hear them or not, for that was simply not where her mind was. She just had to have him, every aching thrust of his cock pressing up against her innermost barrier, though Darren never thrust so hard that it felt uncomfortable for her, as if something unwanted was bearing up inside her.

The dominant leopard simply knew her body that well, knew how far he could go, exactly what angle of his hips would allow him to get that succulent extra touch of penetration to bury his entire shaft inside her. Maybe that was why he had always been renowned as a stud of a lover back in their university days together, even before Evie had snapped him up for herself in their final year of studying.

Things worked out for the best, but never, not back then, would Evie have anticipated being laid out on the balcony to be bred, knowing that the next stage in their lives was to begin, together. Heat coursed through her as she ached and tingled, her mind pulled from one sensation to the next, almost as if her body did not know what it wanted to see through at any one time. Her toes curled, thighs contracting, yet not even that bunching of muscle and power would ever have been enough to push her stud leopard off her.

She climaxed suddenly, a burst of white-hot heat clawing at her, breaking a yowl from her lips. And yet Evie was not in her right mind, not in that moment, not with orgasm bearing through her, ripping and curling, twisting deep to draw up even the tiniest pulses of pleasure that she would never before have considered existing. The hardness of the decking under them bore up against a calf and the leopardess was dimly aware that she had slipped off one of the flat cushions that he had laid down for her. not that that was going to be anywhere near enough to get her to ask him to stop, not when his barbed pole filled her so perfectly.

"Unff... Mmmph..."

Evie couldn't get out anything that at all sounded like words from her lips, though she didn't care, not as he claimed her, stroke after stroke powering into her pussy, stretching her out, a low growl pulling at the back of her throat. Maybe she was just feral, in that moment, letting him take her, waking something more primal, those deepest, most buried of instincts that anthros so very seldomly let out to play.

And yet she would, coming back to herself just a little bit more as she clenched around him, massaging his cock with her pussy, aching for him as much as he wanted her. His eyes locked onto her, seeming so much lighter in the tangible darkness of his dark-furred muzzle, though the halo of his mane did not denote Darren as any angel. She wound her fingers tightly into the mane at the back of his neck as he pressed his lips to hers and claimed her mouth once more in a kiss.

His tongue darted forth, taking what was its own, sweeping around her mouth and curling up against hers in a way that would have had Evie swooning if she had been at all upright. But she was not upright, not then, not with him powering into her, the slop of her sexual fluids slickening the path of his cock. Yet there was still delightful friction there, enough to have her bucking and arching eagerly up against him, passion rising through at the delectable peak of it all.

They needed it and it was time for them to move on, together, to the next chapter of their lives. She panted, pressing up closer, though it was his barbs that stimulated her to another orgasm, flashing before her eyes, skin crawling with illicit pleasure, his hind paw smacking back against the balcony barrier, which was a solid one, thankfully. He was getting there too, she knew that much, though it was not for Evie to dictate, not as she allowed the moment to sweep her away, safe and secure in the knowledge that she could ride out as many orgasms as Darren was willing to give her, her bare, heat-swollen pussy impaled on his breeding spire.

"Unff… My leopardess…"

His paw cupped her face as he just barely broke the kiss, but that was not what the moment was about. He powered into her, stroke after stroke, claiming her body as his own even as his barbs pulled through her, bringing the leopardess, yet again, to the brink of another orgasm. She panted heavily, a yowl playing on her lips, but it was when he plunged suddenly as deep as he could go, trembling against her, that she knew it had come.

His roar blasted forth, echoing across the side of the building and beyond, swept away by the rising wind, though there was no one, at least in sight, there to hear them. It at least let them believe that the moment was there and their own, theirs to take as they pleased, lust pounding, driving them on, thrust after thrust, power and passion trembling forth with the very best of them. Together, they ploughed passionately straight on into orgasm together, every spurt of cum flowing into her bare pussy, unprotected, right when she was in the depths of her heat.

There was no going back from a moment like that and never would Evie want to as she pressed passionately up to him, quivering, her tail finding his and brushing up against it. And yet the leopardess was still borne down in the mating place under his might and power, knowing exactly where she was, what she was to be doing, grunting and groaning, letting passion sweep through. Her pussy clenched around him but she was no more in control of her body than she ever was – much less than when she merely handed it over into Darren's ever-loving, softly dominating paws.

He stayed there, burying deep, their heated breath mingling, yet there was no more perfect moment to cap off their first breeding, his cock spending every drop into her bare pussy. It flowed deep, seeking her eggs within, the cubs that would be born in the months to come after fertilisation. Yet that was for them, their next journey, Evie purring softly, her body aching deliciously in the warmth of the afterglow, though her heat urged her on to more, so much more.

Soon, she told it. Soon, it would have what it wanted.

In that moment, however, all she wanted to do was to lie with her partner, to enjoy it, to relax where they were, knowing that all was right with their little corner of the world, the world that they had made for themselves.

In breeding passion, their lives had only come even closer together than before.

Taking it Deeper

Backdoor Play

"Are you sure you're ready for this?"

Nick chewed a bit nervously at the inside of his cheek, but he was the kind of dragon to wait and wait and wait until he could have done the thing that he wanted to be sure about a hundred times over before going for it. He liked to be sure, even more so when it came to others and the love of his life too, Iris: a beautiful gryphon anthro with pink feathers and a rich, ruby bottom half of fur, the tip of her feline-like tail thickly furred with matching, pink fluff.

He sat back on the bed, shaking his head, even as Iris stepped up with a gleam in her purple eyes and a rather large dildo in her hands. Her tail lashed back and forth, easily betraying her excitement, even as she looked down at the big dragon on the bed, his white scales so familiar to her, though it was the speckling of blue running down his back, keeping close to his spine, that she really adored on him. It was one of his defining features, the points of his body, such as his horns and the horn-like protrusions at the tips of his wings, a similar shade of light blue, catching the light.

"Oh, Nick," she crooned, tipping forward, the two of them naked, though his eyes could not help but drop to her breasts with a low, throaty groan. "You worry too much, really... Just relax. There's nothing to worry about here, I promise. I want to do this! I don't know why you wanted to make me take bigger toys first, but I'm here to show you that I'm more than ready to take *you*!"

Iris grinned, fluttering her pink wings faintly, though she had her partner's attention already. She wasn't so sure why she was the more forward one in the relationship, but that didn't mean at all that she adored Nick any the less – it was just how he was. She wouldn't have felt herself to be very much of a partner at all if she had not loved him like that. But she didn't come to his place that night to think about things like that.

Oh no... No, what Iris had been craving was something a little different, a gryphoness who adored sexual experimentation, always trying something new, though she loved coming back to old favourites too, certain positions and the like that made her heart pound and her body ache wonderfully. But she'd wanted to try anal, which she hadn't thought would be all that different for Nick – and yet the dragon had worried more than she had anticipated about hurting her.

He did, she reflected, have rather a big cock, though. That was good, though it lay, soft, against his thigh where he sat on his wide bed, the dragon hungrily looking her up and down, though his fingers curled into the edge of the bed, as if he didn't quite know what to do. But that was alright when she was there and ready, even with her tail hole already well-lubricated (that was why she had taken so long in the bathroom) to show him that she was more than ready to feel him inside her anal passage.

Nick gulped as the gryphoness sashayed up to him, swinging her hips lustfully, setting the toy on the bed for the moment.

"Don't you want to feel it too, darling?" She breathed, raising her eyebrows, the thicker ridges of feathers above her eyes that gave her delicate face more expression. "How *tight* I'm going to be back there? It's different from pussy, I think... That's what I read online anyway. But I really want to feel you in there, ridges popping in and out, gently stretching me out."

Leaning in close, she draped her arms around his neck, pecking a kiss onto his muzzle. Her breasts brushed his chest and, against himself, Nick groaned.

"Iris…"

"I know what I do to you," she murmured, tail flicking back and forth, simply unable to keep it still. "And I really want to do more to you, darling. It's going to be fine, you don't have to worry about me so much. We'll go nice and slow though and stop anytime that you're not happy with anything, okay?"

Nick shook his head, but not in disagreement with taking it slowly.

"No… I mean, yes, I want to try it too, I just don't want to hurt you."

"You *won't* hurt me, darling, I promise. But thank you for thinking of me so much. I don't know what I'd do if I didn't have you in my life."

They kissed, the dragon automatically tilting his head to the side so that he could better lock his muzzle with her beak, kissing her deeply, letting their tongues tangle and gently lap up against one another. For a kiss like that could say more than a thousand words spilt from the heart as she pressed in close and he snuck his tail between her legs, rubbing it back and forth against her pussy in just the way that she liked.

The effect on the gryphon was electric, Iris arching her back, grinding down onto his tail. She moaned into his mouth and Nick doubled down on his efforts, letting her take as much or as little as she wanted from him, his cock stirring, throbbing with a little more life. It ached to be hard again and the closeness of her body and the depth of the kiss helped him forget his overly prominent concerns about harming her. Arousal helped with that, his cock fleshing out, showing the light ridges that spiralled around his cock, no other quite like it, he was sure, in the world. But that could have been said about any body, truly.

"Please..." Iris breathed, breaking the kiss with some obvious regret. "I want to show you I can do this. And put on a little bit of a show for you, honey..."

He grinned, unable to say no to her, her breasts pressed to his chest as she rolled against him, mischief in her gaze.

"Go on then," Nick murmured, huskier than ever, tail rubbing lightly against her sex, trying to catch her clit for a little extra stimulation. "I'd love to see you, sweetie... I bet you're going to look even hotter."

Iris chirped happily. Oh, that was exactly what she had wanted to hear! Grabbing the toy, she slipped back where she had ended up practically in his lap, her backside clenching eagerly. Oh, it was time, yes, it was, and she needed to show it, a wiggle in her hips accentuated by the sway of her tail.

"I can't wait for you to see," she breathed, turning around and bending a little, waggling her tail a little higher to show off her round backside. "I'm going to make you want to pounce on me and fuck me, darling..."

The dragon let out an appreciative groan, though she could barely weight to show him. The toy was big, but with a smooth length and a defined head with a rounded tip that was easy to get into herself, despite its size. She'd had to work up to it, to be fair, when she was taking care, but there was simply something about anal penetration that made her heart pound and her orgasms...wow. She didn't even know how to describe the orgasms she'd had with the smaller toys and that one too!

She worked the toy back and forth, wetting the tip with the dampness from her pussy, her arousal already high. Bending over at the waist, her backside faced her lover, tail flicked up so that everything was on show, wanting him to see everything, not wanting to hide a single note from him.

That wasn't the point of it, not as her breath caught and she pressed the fat, rounded tip of the toy to her anal ring, offering herself to it, grunting softly in the back of her throat.

"Oh, this is going to feel so good…"

She knew it would, and it was even better as she pressed it up into her backside, relaxing around it, even though she wanted to clench. She wanted even more pressure and pleasure as it opened her up and stretched her out, her body aching for it, the dildo pushing deeper and deeper. It was not the most comfortable position for the gryphoness to stand in, tail kept high, though she could not keep the wiggle out of it, but it would have to do. They would really have to invest in a little chair for the bedroom, as small as it was, if they were going to engage in a little voyeuristic play and pleasure more often than not again.

But she could only focus on the toy driving into her, her hand working it deeper and deeper, thrusting and pushing to get it inside. The slickness of the lubricant that she had pre-prepared her body with helped it easily along the way, her body already feeling so very full, aching and pulsing, feeling every beat of her heart and pulse as it pounded through her.

Nick watched, spellbound. The dragon had never thought that it could be anywhere near as hot as it was to watch a partner penetrating themselves like that, adoring their own bodies like that. He'd only briefly watched her masturbating before, but there was something even more hypnotic about her grinding a thick length of silicone dildo deep up into her tail hole. He could even see exactly how tight her anal ring was around the toy, flexing and puckering, though she could not push it out, clearly. Not when the gryphoness was so keen, in a moment just like that, to push it in, to thrust it deeper.

"Oh, Nick..." She moaned for him, tongue flickering out over the edge of her beak. "It feels so good... Mmmm... I just wish it was your cock."

The dragon groaned, but he couldn't help himself. His hands were up and on her backside in the blink of an eye. She murmured as he squeezed, kneading her flesh, almost getting in her way, but he couldn't stop himself, caught in Iris' spell.

"What do you do to me, Iris?" He growled, lust rising, cock aching, throbbing to full hardness with a droplet of pre-cum clinging to the tip. "Fuck... You make me... Mmm..."

He couldn't articulate quite what she made him do, all the blood in his body rushing to exactly the right-wrong places. Not that the dragon cared, not as he stared at her hungrily, need rising within him, doubts fading. It was such a big toy that he could barely understand just how she took it, but that suddenly didn't matter anymore. Iris was just there to show him that she could take it, that she was every bit the hot, sexy gryphoness that she naturally was, that he didn't always have to be there looking after her, looking over her shoulder.

That he could let go and have his fun with her too...

She chirped, the toy pushing deep, tail flicking high, though Iris could not hide how her pussy dripped and drooled, so slick and wet that it was practically splattering between her legs. It was not her fault that her body was so over productive, that she got so wet and ready, something that previous boyfriends had complained about. But it was just the way that the gryphon and her body were, throwing herself whole-heartedly into it.

It felt good, too good, bearing down so that the full length of the thick dildo ground into her, though she wanted more. It warmed to the heat of her body, but she wanted more, the heat of her lover's cock inside her, whimpering, grunting, twisting her head back and forth.

The dragon's tail snaked up between her legs, teasing her clit, the folds of her pussy, but it was just a tease, riling her up even more, all to the point where she barely even thought she could think straight. Iris moaned, wings fluttering over her back, though she needed the firm hold of her lover right there and then, right at the point that her legs went weak.

"Mmm, I got you..."

And then Nick was there, using his tail to support her around her belly while he stood and pressed in close to her back. With the drake grinding against her rump, his cock hard and ready, aching for similar delight, she didn't need to hold herself up anymore or the dildo, the toy ground as deeply up inside her backside as it was possible to be.

But the dragon was taking control, her stomach churning into delicious knots, winding itself up, her breath caught in her throat, tight in her chest. Yet all in the best of ways, curls of anticipation flowing through her, aching desperately, wanting, groaning.

"Come here, sweetie," Nick growled, the dragon holding the base of the dildo, giving it a few experimental pumps, twisting his hand. "I want you... If you want this, you can control the pace."

Nothing could have made her heart leap quite like that, the dragon drawing the toy out of her backside, only to grind his cock up and under her tail. He groaned, which only enticed her even more, feeling as if she was on the edge of climax already, needing it, whimpering for it, losing herself to it.

She'd never been one to take the top position, after all, even though Iris was more than happy to take the lead.

That was just why it was easy for her to allow Nick to draw her back as he sat on the bed, his knees together to settle her in his lap. Yet there was the throbbing length of meat to delve into her tail hole first, the tip prying at her gaping pucker, already well-prepared for his lust.

Nick grunted, but he wouldn't go back now that he had begun, licking his lips, eyes fixed on her buttocks, watching the prod of his cock, how her body rocked back against him, wanting it.

"Yes, please... Ohhh..." Iris moaned. "I want it... Please, Nick, please..."

He would not deny her and Iris could not help but trill as his thick, ridged length sank into her. It might have been slower than she would have liked, but that was more than fine, as long as they both got what they wanted, as long as they shared the pleasure.

"Unff... Ohh..."

Yet Iris could not help her cries of pleasure as she sank onto her partner's cock, taking the dragon's dick deep. It was so much better than a toy, hot and warm and drooling pre-cum, though she took it slower, the thickness teasingly stretching her out even wider.

The dragon grinned, getting into it, the exquisite tightness wrapped around his cock, though he did not thrust, bearing down into the carpet with his feet, enjoying the moment, grunting thickly, leaning in close. His arms slid around her naturally as she pushed down to take the full length of his dick into her slick tail hole, holding her in place, holding her hips, guiding her up and down, even though it was still mostly the gryphoness setting the pace.

"Fuck, sweetie," he puffed, needing more breath than he was actually getting into his lungs. "Mmmph, you're so damn hot like this!"

He needed a little more to get into the moment than Iris, as had been shown multiple times over, but that only made it even sweeter when they came together on the right wavelength. And they reached the delicious depths of that increasingly frequently as they learned the ins and outs of one another sexually, how to best please the other, confident in themselves and their partner. Some partners just took a little longer to find their rhythm with each other and that was okay too.

It was worth it for how they came together, the gryphoness grunting with little puffs of breath as she rode his cock, grinding down, finding the angles that worked for her, though the tightness was more than enough for him. Nick growled, drawing her in tight to his chest, a hand on her breast, squeezing, tweaking her nipple, all while his tail curled around to rub her clit, the front of her pussy that he could reach.

"Cum for me," he growled, losing himself there, nipping at her neck. "God, you're so beautiful... Mmph, so tight!"

It was much tighter than fucking her pussy, dropping into cruder language even in his own mind, panting heavily. If he had been able to sweat he would be doing so, though all Nick could do, as a reptile, was hang his jaws open to allow excess heat to dissipate from his body. Her backside squeezed around him as Iris moaned and rode him, rocking back and forth, aching for it as much as he was. Yet she didn't seem to know whether to push into his tail or back onto his cock, caught up in a delicious conundrum of lust.

Iris whimpered, so close to climax, yet content to let Nick get her there. He had to be close too, his balls throbbing, loins aching to spend his load, but she would slam down on him and grind into his lap as soon as she climaxed, waiting for that moment. Panting heavily, her breasts rolled into the grasp of his hand, her body eager for it, drooling over his tail, the cord of tightness drawing tauter and tauter within her core until her body could hold it back for not a heartbeat more.

She cried out, bucking and grinding, shoving her hips all the way down, on his lap. Iris' cries filled the bedroom, her arse tight on his cock, clenching around the base, though the dragon was only a breath behind. With a deep, low groan that seemed to draw itself out from the depths of his being, the dragon filled her, shaking his head back and forth, struggling in the moment to control his lust even when he could let go fully. He still had his partner in mind, holding her tightly to him, longing and loving, even as pulses of ecstasy coursed through him.

"Unff... Fuck... Iris..."

She didn't hear him, pushing down on his shaft, moaning, losing herself as she creamed on his tail, leaving a slick mess that, later, they would wash off in the shower together. It was too good to be filled, to be stretched out to that extent, though Iris very much hoped that it was an anal experience that would be repeated in the future – very soon, if she had her way about it!

Yet they settled there, heaving and panting in grunting pleasure, Iris riding it out until she had milked her climax of every last pulse and ripple, muscles clenching down on nothing in her pussy and too much in her backside. His cum drooled out of her tail hole, despite the stretch, ridges pressing up against the right places inside her, stimulating her, making her want it all over again, even though that would probably be enough for one night.

"Mmmm..."

Relaxing a little, she leaned back against him, letting his arms hold her safe and warm, tail flicking back against her dragon's scales. Nick murmured something to her that she did not quite catch, but that didn't matter. They would kiss and cuddle and the aftercare to sex would almost prove to be as great as the sex itself, her whole body tingling and prickling all over with the heat of her passionate orgasm.

Still, she hoped Nick would be just as keen to take her deeper next time, his cock softening inside her backside, cum drooling out thickly. The dragon laid back on the bed, kissing her neck and shoulder, arms tight around her, squeezing lightly.

"I love you so much…"

Squirming in his lap, lying on top of him, Iris giggled faintly.

"Love you too, sweetheart… Now, when can we do it again?"

The dragon's answer, when it came, made her heart soar.

"Anytime you like, sweetie, I promise. Anytime."

Slowly but surely, Nick would become more adventurous, trusting himself not to push his lover too far.

Communication, after all, would always lead them right.

Lust in the Surf

The mare lay flat on the surfboard, a damp rash vest clinging to her torso while her board shorts dried in the warm summer sun. Her red coat glowed faintly with good health, but the sprinkling of salt crystals in her chestnut fur would later need to be washed out, cleansed from her hair so that it would not dry wispy and tangled. It was more than a fair exchange for a day out on the water, however, a smile on her lips while she floated, waiting on the right wave.

Not that one. It had not risen into something rideable, and she pushed off, kicking and paddling with her arms, ducking under it. One moment she was in the open air and the next she was in an underwater world, her eyes open, the shape of the wave moving above her. It was a strange, otherworldly position to find herself in, yet the underwater world cut her off from all other realities on the edge of the Cornish coastline, foam breaking, the ocean flowing around her.

Garnet smiled. It was, truly, one of the best places to be.

She broke the surface again with a gasp, even though she had not been under the surface of the water for all that long, mane soaked again and clinging to her neck. There was no time, however, to brush it aside as a more rideable wave approached, moments ticking by as the swell grew and grew. Lines of white foam, bubbles driven by the break of the waves, rushed towards the base of the swell as she turned and paddled furiously, her back to it, arms scooping through the water powerfully, forcing the board along in the same direction.

Come on...

There would always be a chance, a small chance, that one would not catch a wave, even when it had been carefully chosen. Yet that was not the case in that instance with Garnet's board pointed back to the beach, scattered with the brightly coloured summer clothing and hides of furs. She knew some of them that were there, but couldn't identify them from that distance, the wave catching, pushing – and then lifting her up and along in a moment of rushing weightlessness.

Yes!

It had happened, yet she was not a passive player in the ride as she pressed her palms close to the edge of the board, testing her strength. The fibreglass was waxed and ready as she popped up, pushing off with her arms at the same time as her lower body snapped up under her, hooves catching her weight. Not the easiest move to pull off but possible with the pop of her body, quick and decisive.

And then she was up and riding the wave, cutting across the face as she directed the board, a wild cry breaking her lips as she struck through. It was hers and no one else's, other surfers drifting aside, though she could more than easily carve a winding path through them if she so chose. They were not coming for the same ride as her, however, as she whipped the board at the peak of the wave, cresting with white water.

Alas, even if the swell was a good four or five foot out there, it was not the kind that could be found in the tropics and broke into white water too soon. Yet that was even more intoxicating, in a way, pushing her on with the pounding force of a hundred white horses, all ablaze in a charge for the shoreline. The froth and foam of the blistering white water leapt and cavorted around her as she let its strength carry her onward, the beach beckoning, shallower water playing with the underside of her board.

Too soon, the wave lost strength, fading, weakening, until it dropped her off, rushing by without any energy left to carry her. It may have swept up further on the shore, leaving another tide mark on the beach, but it would return to the ocean again, all the same, flowing back, softening into the entirety of it that could not so easily be forgotten.

Salt lingered on her lips as she hopped off the board with a splash, wet through with the ankle bad keeping her connected to the board in case of any unscheduled dismounts from the ride. With thirst clawing at her throat, she headed to shore, the board tucked up under her arm, a heavy load to carry but not so when she had it balanced just right. Garnet chuckled faintly to herself, sweeping her forelock back from her eyes so that she could see a little better. The only problem with carrying a longboard, of course, was turning quickly. She'd taken out more than one small child with inattention before and probably would again.

"Hey, hun."

Andy sat up, setting his e-reader aside, the screen adjusted to be seen more easily in bright sunshine. The blue-furred wolf, not being one for the water, was shirtless, alluringly so, and relaxed in the warm bath of the sunshine caressing his fur, laziness ringing through every muscle in his body, despite the activity of others around him. Although the beach was not the busiest around, it still attracted a fair number of tourists off the coast of Cornwall and that's exactly why they were on holiday too – tourists looking for their own kind of break from reality, the grind and drudgery of real life.

Maybe more furs in the world would be happier if they weren't constantly looking for an escape.

Grabbing a drink from the cool box, the mare threw it back, glugging thirstily, suddenly so desperate for it that she couldn't get it all down her throat quickly enough. Funny how things like that worked, so keen to be out on the water for so long and then forgetting to take care of her basic needs despite thinking vaguely about them. But the ocean was not something that, all so often, she got to enjoy.

"Phew!" She sighed, breathing a little more easily with her thirst quenched. "The waves are great out there. You've really got to come out and join me sometime."

But the wolf knew that she was joking, slouching back, sunglasses on, the purple of his hair fluffed up between his ears from the sea and the sand. Although the white of his stomach was on show, topless and comfortable, his thicker fur did make staying out in the sun for too long a little more difficult than it was for her.

"You always say that, but you know it's not happening."

She laughed, shaking her head.

"Yeah, yeah, I know that, but I'll never stop inviting you to come out with me. Besides, there're some fine studs out there, I'm sure you'd like chasing that tail…"

She cast him a sly look out of the corner of her eye that was anything but coy, the wolf's eyes impassive behind his shades. However, the smirk on his lips was not something that was so easily concealed, even then.

"Mm, there's plenty up here to look at too…"

Garnet rolled her eyes. Dogs. Weren't they all the same? She chuckled softly, towelling off her mane and her tail, knowing that his eyes were on her as much as they were on the other furs on the beach, passing by, enjoying their days. Summer was a time to show both fur and scales – feathers too, if one was of that inclination – but the board shorts clung to her backside, showing off her shape, as much as wearing nothing at all may have done.

She straightened, eyes hungrily latched back onto the sparkling ocean, how the water danced and played, inviting her back.

"There's a good swell coming in," she said, casting the words back over her shoulder even as his tail twitched, eyes all on her that time. "I'll stay out another hour, come back in. Dinner at that restaurant we passed on the way in tonight, hm, wuff?"

He nodded, though him turning to the side, hiding something over his crotch, told more of a tale than his grunt, though Garnet grinned, hardly able to blame him for his condition, if it could even be called that. There'd been far, far too much going on over recent months and the exhaustion of turmoil, struggling through, could not be held back for too long. Whereas she needed to refresh away from the digital world, if all he needed to do was to sprawl on the beach and soak up the rays, that was all fine with her too.

The water beckoned her, paddling out, the waves trying to push her back into shore as she ducked under the ones that she could, once the water was deep enough. Keeping to the right side of the beach, away from the reef that sent choppy water coursing forth, she paddled at the edge of the lifeguard's flags, though she knew where the currents were on that stretch of beach. There, the lifeguards set the flags so that they only had a section of water to watch rather than a wider span. With so many out there who were not as familiar with the water as she was, she couldn't blame them, though it did restrict the scope of the water that she was, at least there, permitted to surf.

It was peaceful on the edge, however, paddling out, letting the lull of the swell soothe her, rocking her board. Only one other was near and she hadn't been lying to Andy when she'd mentioned that there were some rather fetching figures out there, for the leanly muscled stallion had caught her eye from the beginning.

She didn't hide her looks, licking her lips, hips shifting. A strong body would draw anyone's eye as his mane drifted on the back of his neck, half-dry as if it had been a while side his last ride, but her eyes roamed down his body. The line of his spine demanded attention down to his buttocks, wearing similar board shorts in a popular brand, but his appaloosa-spotted coat hinted at a blanket covering to his buttocks and upper thighs. The bulk of his coat was black, shiny with the water and sunshine, but those flecks of white made her want to pull them down, to see the patterning – and more – that lay beneath.

"See something you like, babe?"

It could have been something due an eye roll under any other circumstance, but a surfer's twang strung out through his tone, betraying casual laziness to everything. And that laziness was not a bad thing, not when the haste of the world pushed at everyone, demanding more, reminding furs like that very stallion that there was still more to be had from life than making the rat race, in some way, work for them.

"What do you think?"

She countered with her own smile, eyebrow raised, tail flicking up as if in invitation. A little flirt and a tease, however, was all well and good, but they were as good as two wild horses appraising each other out in the wild, far away from anyone, seeking out a partner that was on the same wavelength as them.

He grinned easily, teeth flashing between his lips, though her heart skipped a beat. Sitting up, Garnet swung her legs over the side of the board, letting them dangle, playing through the life-flow of the water, always moving.

"Not many come out this far," he said, one ear flicking towards her. "You must be a strong surfer."

Chuckling, she shook her head, though that was not a denial of him.

"You could say, good enough for the water out here, surely, but you wouldn't catch me trying to take on bigger surf than this. This kinda swell I can handle."

"Then what else can you handle?"

He was bold, so bold, but her grin only widened, matching his.

Oh, yes…

"Why don't you come over here and find out?"

Her tail tried to lift but that was difficult to do while she was sitting on it, the stallion incoming, swimming strongly with just his arms. He was toned but not overly muscled, perfectly for a surfer, though she didn't need to know his background to know that he spent a lot of time out on the water. There was a peace to that kind of fur, the type that took time out away from work, and there were few past times more separating from the world that others wanted you to think was the only one than taking to water instead of land.

Back on the beach, she knew that her boyfriend was there, the wolf waiting for her, reading his book or watching the eye candy strut by. She knew that even as her fingers caressed the stallion's muzzle, welcoming him closer, her free paw splayed flat on his chest, the stud slipping into the water and pulling her with him. Amongst the light swells, no waves incoming that were rideable for the moment, their bodies made hardly anything of a ripple, her lips meeting his.

Well, he should have come out with me if he wanted to do more than look.

She moaned keenly into his mouth, heart pounding, the lust of the moment pushing her on, driving her as if it was a wave that she was catching, feeling it lift her. Yet she was no more a passive player in that moment than she was when riding a wave, their tongues tangling, lust rising, pushing up against one another as if, suddenly, there was nothing else that existed in the world for either of them.

It was a moment, a moment that would come and pass, but she didn't need to even know his name, not to lust for him. Her body prickled with lazy heat, though there was nothing lazy about what she planned to do out there on the water, groaning softly, clinging to him as if to stay afloat. The mare's board threatened to drift away as she panted softly, nostrils fluttering with greedy sucks of breath, though it was not as if he could hide his lust for her too.

"Ohhh…" He moaned, their lips broken, parted between them, a string of saliva connecting them only briefly while the waves lapped up around. "Didn't think… Mmmph… You'd go that far."

But it was all in good fun, her paw dropping, trusting him to hold her up, his lips on her throat, nibbling and nipping, teasing yet another throaty grunt from her lips. It was a moment, yet a moment that stretched out in the gentle lap of the ocean, drifting with their boards further from the flags, although the water was calmer there. Maybe the swell that she'd seen coming was more spaced out than she'd realised or maybe it had faded over the reef, but none of that mattered as Garnet's paw squeezed the growing length of his cock through his board shorts.

She smirked, dropping a kiss on his nose, turning her back to him only to arch it, grinding onto his shaft. Her shorts hid little, even as they floated lightly around her thighs in the lack of gravity of the ocean, rump teasing his prick until the tip slipped higher, threatening to push from the waistband of his shorts.

"Ohhh…"

His groans were wonderful, enough to make her keep pushing on, teasing and flirting, flagging her tail as he tugged his shorts down, freeing his prick in a spring of fleshy meat. The grey length was lightly speckled with pink, though she would not see that until later, the thick pole sliding over her backside as if it already knew just where it was that it wanted to go.

Garnet nickered, throat trembling lightly, his paws at her hips, their boards drifting, bobbing, the mere act and art of surfing forgotten. It was okay, all okay, though she was sure she'd have quite a tale to tell the wolf once she returned to shore, even if he might have a few choice words and a hard, dripping prick for her while she teased him about it. With the appaloosa's lips on her neck, she grunted, head awash with her own brand of lust. What was a little fun, after all, out on the water?

She groaned, the stallion pressed to her back, legs kicking under the water, only enough to stop them putting too much pressure on their boards, though the stallion's board was liable to drift away with only one of his paws resting too heavily on it. They were close, so close, yet they had to remember where they were, the shore too far away to return to swiftly in an emergency. Yet it was that very added edge of danger that had her leaning over her board, letting him come right along with her as water swilled over the top side of the board, slipping between the patterns in the wax before the entire body of it was submerged.

She gasped, his fingers tugging her shorts down, though only enough to free her backside, his fingers hungrily seeking out her pussy, though the wetness of her folds was lost in the ocean. Yet she nickered for it, demanding it all, his finger sliding into her while his thumb brushed her clit, the natural flow of the ocean aiding their passion.

"Mmm..." She moaned, cheek pressed to the board, abs aching from holding her torso up. "Come on, stud, you can do better than that. If you don't do something...unff...proper soon, I'll head back to the beach and see if the lifeguard wants to see how a real mare rides in the changing rooms..."

But it seemed that he had no intention whatsoever of doing that, fingers working deep inside as she snorted, pushing over her, trusting the board to retain its buoyancy, the flat surface not enough to support both of their bodies at once, as much as they may have liked it. Not in the throes of passion, at least, another finger added to the first, sliding into her slickness as she slipped her ears back.

She, of course, had no intention of going elsewhere when she had a stallion right there to take her cheeky pleasure with, body burning up with need as he whuffled at her shoulder, trying to reach the back of her neck. But he had to pull her back off the board, his hardness demanding attention that she was only too willing to give, facing him and closing her hand lightly around his shaft.

"What...this?" She smirked, kissing his lips fleetingly, so quickly that he didn't have a moment in which to react. "Mmm, I think you've got something pretty thick...needing something. Just like any stud."

He grunted, losing a little of his relaxed demeanour, grumbling something about him not being just any stud, but it was hard for him to worry about something like that when a mare's paw was on his dick. She squeezed his length behind the head, paw gliding down seamlessly, teasing over the medial ring, playing with his sheath at the base. His nuts did not receive the tease that they could have at such a time, her legs going around his waist, trusting him to support her weight in the water as she let go of the board.

It was an act of faith and trust all at once, but it had to come as his prick pressed up to her pussy. She couldn't get him inside her if she clung to the board, though he held onto his behind her back, the two of them getting turned around somehow. Garnet's arm slung around the appaloosa stallion's shoulders, the tip of his cock pressing up to the folds of her pussy while she fed him into her.

The board tugged at her fetlock, connected by the leg strap, but did not drift away as she sank onto him, taking his shaft inside her cunny, inch after fat inch. It spread her open in just the right way, just the right amount, not too big and most certainly, being a stallion, not too small. They groaned in unison, her arms going around both his neck and shoulders at once, letting him kick and kick, thrusting lightly with the natural motion of his body, though it was her that controlled the depth. For her legs tightened around him, hooves digging into buttock and thigh, rising and falling on his shaft, taking him deeper and deeper, her head falling back in the delight of the moment.

No one else. Not even her boyfriend. Oh, he could not know what he was doing out there, but she imagined the cucked wolf eyeing her up, binoculars pressed up to his face, though it was all fine for the two of them, just another story to tell later. But he could not remain in her mind while the stud of a stallion grunted and snorted before her, eyes intense, such a shade of blue that she'd never seen on another equine before, trying to kiss her even as they struggled to maintain any semblance of breath.

No words. Grunted groans, heaving moans. Yes, those were the language of lust between them as water slapped their necks, waves picking up, a little choppier than they should have been, the sun having moved across the sky into the mid-afternoon. The day was getting on but there were no eyes on them, not then, their bodies clad in the swell of the ocean, a bigger wave that would break closer to shore lifting them, boards coming along.

It was safe for them, at least then, the stallion clinging to the board, though the edge of it jutted uncomfortably into her shoulder blades, dipping to her upper back when it tilted a little too much. But that was no matter to them, not either of them, for the most passionate of moments were not always destined to be the most comfortable. Maybe that was why they had both, at least then and there, decided to throw caution to the sky and the sea, taking their lust and pleasure together as he throbbed thickly inside her.

The need to stay afloat meant that they could not come together too passionately, his thrusts muted and more from the need of him kicking and pushing to keep them up at the surface. For the horse didn't just need to keep himself afloat but her and the board too, or else the moment would become a whole lot less sexy very quickly.

Garnet smirked, kissing his nose, capturing his lips as she sank, tightening her grip on him, hardly letting him thrust, though a kind of feral instinct still bid him to. She saw the strain in his eyes, the need in him, imagining just how his balls were throbbing at that very moment even though she couldn't take them in her paw and feel for herself.

But that was alright. That was just a little trade-off for another kind of lust for her to indulge in, a moment where she could take it for her own, remember it, tongues tangling, sweeping up against one another. All that the mare had to do was savour the hot length of stallion-cock throbbing inside her, the tip flaring a little more, closer and closer to cumming with every passing second.

Not yet though, not yet. Just a little longer, a little bit longer, they could enjoy themselves out there. There was no rush, bar the oncoming tide, and the seconds could stretch out as she moaned into his mouth, twisting her fingers into his mane without thinking, dragging him to her even more fervently than before.

Yes... Yes, sometimes, it was moments like that which were needed. He could not help but thrust, grinding deeper inside her, the shift of his hips and thighs pushing him against her. Her breasts squashed lightly to his chest, nipples softly showing through the soaked fabric of her rash vest and even the bikini top underneath too, though it was never designed to conceal anything. Out on the water, times like that were supposed to be for surfing, for relaxing, the play of the ocean. Perhaps not so much what they were using it for, as much as they leaned into it.

Passion, however, could not be held back for all that long, her hips working, finding a rhythm again, tensing her abs. Oh, how the mare would ache later, but the passion headed it off, throwing all manner of strain from the act of lust away, far away. It did not matter with his length inside her, grinding on him, his shaft pressing up against her clit as she angled her hips just right, though his paw down between their bodies, teasing it directly, would have been even better.

Maybe later...

For there were still options open as she moaned, rocking on him, panting heavily through flared nostrils, lips brushing, tongues flickering together, though the kiss was sloppier and sloppier as they sank in the water. She strained, tightening her grip on him even further, clenching down as much as she felt able to, her sex squeezing around him as muscles worked just to keep her lifted and breathing while more and more of his pre-cum drooled into her.

The stallion snorted against her shoulder and she knew it would not be long, the pressure within her lower abdomen building and building, snorting heavily, pressing against him.

So close…

Garnet heaved, head thrown back, bumping the board, though that little knock was still not enough to dissuade her as she muffled her orgasm the best she could, ears twitching, hips working furiously. The water splashed up more vehemently around them than ever as they moaned in unison, his head sinking, water tickling at her ears, though orgasm tore through her with the raw power of a tidal wave. Such was the force that could not be stopped as she took his cock, her sex pulsing erratically around him, muscular twitches at that point of blissful ecstasy beyond her control, desire throbbing deeply through her.

She arched against him and one of his paws lustfully dropped, squeezing her arse as he climaxed too, one hard thrust of his hips dropping them both underwater while he spent his load, clinging to one another. They may have been barely under the surface but maybe there was something about air deprivation, even then, that made it most erotic, something exotic that could not be gleaned in any other moment, orgasms pounding forth, stretching out. For she felt every juddering stroke of his cock inside her, driving and pounding, aching as it pumped her full of seed that would, very soon, be washed away by the ocean.

Alas, breath had to be caught up with at some moment, Garnet pushing up with him, her paws scrabbling for his board along with him, bodies twisted together to the side, gasping and clinging to it. Barely aware that they were breathing again, they hung onto it for dear life, the stallion quivering against her, grunting and moaning, eyes half-lidded with lust.

They stayed there, his shaft still inside her, spending forth spurt after spurt of cum, proving his virility (or perhaps that he hadn't gotten off in a while), as he stayed hard. It was the perfect moment, chests heaving for breath, lips close, touched with salt but only lightly brushing up against one another, sun on the waves and a stronger swell of waves pulling at the horizon. They would have to come apart as they teased down from their respective highs, but there was something about coming together as mare and stallion in a moment like that which was hard to pull away from.

They had time. Only a little, the lifeguards finally taking note of them, the jeep in motion, but they had some time. Snorting, the stallion bumped his nose into her neck, drops of seawater clinging to his whiskers.

"Name's Cam," he grunted, head barely above the water as he kicked and she held onto a board to keep them afloat, his hooves kicking. "Want to meet up again later?"

Garnet grinned, dropping a kiss on his cheek, his dick still throbbing inside her. Any evidence of their tryst would be washed away, but she had no intention at all of keeping it a secret. No... Oh no. Her wolf would want every sordid little detail while his nose was crammed between her thighs later that night, scooping his tongue up inside her in the hope that he could tease out a little more of what had taken place there, without him.

"I think so... And I think I have someone that I want you to meet too."

For sharing, of course, was the best part of relationship, was it not?

The stallion blinked, nickering softly, his cock slipping from her, tugging up their shorts as they turned their attention back to their boards. But they would not so easily wipe the memory of that moment from their minds as they grinned, sharing that incident with one another, even if it would blossom into something more, a little something flirtier, all in due course.

The board shorts clung to her folds, like bikini bottoms but more comfortable to move in, a cheeky grin on her lips as they made their way back between the flags. The lifeguards would have to find someone else to bother that day.

"Meet at the Mermaid pub, seven o'clock?"

Cam grinned, licking his lips, though she thought it was an unconscious motion.

"Absolutely, babe."

She shivered. It was going to be an interesting evening indeed.

And there was more to share with her wolf all over again…

Thank you for reading and I hope that everything was very much enjoyed!

Ready for more? Check out my author website for more furry fiction and where you can purchase my books!

https://linktr.ee/amethystmare

Cover art illustrated by verysweetpotato; they are contactable via Twitter for work enquiries.

twitter.com/AlexandrCorvin

www.ingramcontent.com/pod-product-compliance
Lightning Source LLC
Chambersburg PA
CBHW030320080526
44584CB00012B/634